The
Complete Runner's
Day-by-Day
Log and Calendar
1997

The Complete Runner's Day-by-Day Log and Calendar 1997

JOHN JEROME

Random House
New York

ISBN: 0-679-76870-X

Random House website: http://www.randomhouse.com/

Printed in the United States of America

24689753

FIRST EDITION

Designed by Carole Lowenstein

Introduction: Running Through the Post-Running Era

Let's declare this the Post-Running Era. That's all the rage, now, sticking the word "post-" onto the front of one heavy concept after another, or otherwise declaring the end of things. There's even a school of thought that history itself is over and done with, led by American historian Francis Fukuyama, one of whose tracts is actually called *The End of History and the Last Man*.

So okay, running is done for. No more fancy new ultra-lightweight, ultra-long-wearing, ultra-supportive shoe breakthroughs; no more pronating and supinating, no more singlets and skimpy shorts, no more Lycra tights and split times and carbo-loading. Never mind the soaring entry numbers at marathons and 10-Ks; we've obviously gone on to other things. We're out there blade skating and kite skiing and parachuting off office buildings to get our ya-yas. No more low-adrenaline, long-haul sports, no more physiological character building. The human attention span is dwindling as fast as the twentieth century is drawing to a close, and if it ain't on MTV—or better yet, in a fifteen-second commercial containing at least forty-five jump cuts—it doesn't exist.

Besides which, if it can't be done on a video screen, with or without virtual reality technology to make it feel just a little more like real life, it isn't going to make it past the year 2000 anyway. Get with it, runners, or get left behind. We're as anachronistic as wooden sailing ships.

In case it isn't already obvious, the virtual reality business drives me straight up the (solid concrete, real-world) wall. A friend of mine from my wasted youth—we once worked on a car magazine together—claims he recently "won" the Indianapolis 500, via video simulation, while the actual race was going on in real time. I gather he fired up his monitor at the famous command of "Gentlemen (and Lady), start your engines," and finished his simulated two hundred laps before the actual checkered flag was waved at the actual racer.

My friend waxes rhapsodic about the fantastic technological detail possible within his electronic car-racing game. You can change tire pressures and even tire compounds, adjust wing angles, change fuel loadings, adjust boost pressure, attend to all the thousands of details that real-world, big-boy racers have to contend with. The results of these changes actually affect the "handling" (more about that in a moment) and speed and possible lap times of your video race car. You run out of fuel and have to make pit stops. You even get a fairly accurate visual picture (and an aural one; don't forget the noise element) of what it's like to drive around the Indianapolis Motor Speedway at 230 mph. What you don't get is any feeling of what that's like in your gut and your butt and the skin of your face, or through your arms and shoulders: how the car handles, which in my limited experience at driving race cars happened to be where the fun lay.

Ditto golf: someone else sent me a video golf game, in which it is possible to select the course, select the clubs, choose the effort of the swing, even put a little English on the ball at "contact" to curve around that video tree out there in the fairway. Everything about the real game of golf is right there on the disk—

except for the wrists and hands. I don't play golf, but I suspect that the wrists and hands are what it's all about. (And the weather: there are no swirling cross-winds, nor any morning dew on the grass in virtual reality. Or birdsong.)

Athletic virtual reality—*all* of virtual reality, as far as I'm concerned—runs into a wall of its own, I think, at the muscle spindles. It is stopped dead at the level of the proprioceptors, the nerve endings for athletic sensation. Proprioception is the *other* sense—a kind of amalgam of the conventional five—that tells you that you are thus-and-so in relation to the physical world, that at this moment you are in this attitude and at these angles to gravity, that you are moving these muscles in this manner. Proprioception is the body's capacity to tell you you're alive. Virtual reality can't do that.

So anyway we retros—Luddites, techno-dullards, the blue-footed boobies of the information age—are going to be left completely behind. The virtual folks will be quick to point out that there are a hell of a lot easier ways to do this than to get out there on an actual road with our actual, heavy, burdensome bodies.

We're just the saps who actually like to get sweaty, who even enjoy making ourselves tired, who have this stubborn predilection for Actual Reality. (Now *there*'s a concept for you. Something like acoustic guitar, isn't it? Or whole milk?) We're going to be left in the dust, all alone, grinding along on our weary legs, plodding up hill and down, dragging our unwieldy flesh along over actual, five-thousand-two-hundred-and-eighty-foot miles. One after another, until we are all tired out. And won't that be just the ticket? Won't that be nice?

The Complete Runner's Day-by-Day Log and Calendar
1997

JANUARY

S	M	T	W	T	F	S
			1 NEW YEAR'S DAY	2	3	4
5	6	7	8	9	10	11
12	13	14	15	16	17	18
19	20 MARTIN LUTHER KING, JR., DAY	21	22	23	24	25
26	27	28	29	30	31	

January: Inventing the Wheel

Dick Durrance was an American ski racer in the very early days of that sport. He burst on the scene in 1934, after boyhood schooling in the Bavarian Alps, and dominated until World War II put a temporary halt to skiing competition. He was and is a small man, perhaps five-foot-seven at the peak of his racing career, considerably shorter now after a couple of rounds of back surgery. (He'll soon turn eighty-three.) When he was growing up in Garmisch in the late twenties, dreaming of skiing in the 1936 Olympics, he was acutely aware of his physical limitations. He knew he needed to be stronger, and would perform any kind of hard work that came along in the effort to develop himself.

He and his friends found a hidden peak partway up a mountain behind his house, accessible only by rock-climbing, and built a kind of Alpine tree house with a rope ladder on it. He describes the project with relish: "We got a little wagon and would fill it with bricks and rocks and shove it up the slope, eight hundred feet or so to the foot of the chimney, where you had to start to climb. It'd take half an hour to push it up. Then we'd rock-climb to the peak with the bricks in rucksacks. The rock was for a retaining wall so we'd have a flat terrace to build on. When that was done, we'd cut logs and lower them from above."

What counted for Dick wasn't the clubhouse, but the work of building it. He was discovering training—inventing it, in effect, for himself. There was no program laid out for him. He simply took on any task that required severe physical effort, and kept it up as long as he could. He grew up steel-thighed, with legs like tree trunks, and developed a unique low, crouching skiing style that caused some amusement among purists of the day but fit his stature—and won him races. In one of his most famous victories he went off course through a grove of pine trees, hitting one sapling at something like sixty miles per hour. The force knocked him backward so that his hands dragged on the snow behind him, but he had the sheer strength to pull himself back upright, continue, and win.

He never stopped working on that strength. A friend describes him on the morning before a day of on-slope training, stepping up onto a table edge and doing forty-eight one-legged deep-knee bends with each leg before putting on skis. After his ski-racing career he became a filmmaker, and was as famous among his crews for hauling heavy cameras across perilous terrain—on those same steel legs—as he had been as a racer.

What fascinates me about Dick's story is the element of discovery to it. Athletic training was fairly rudimentary in those days, but he wasn't even exposed to what was available. He made it up. He trained by noticing results rather than by following instructions. He wasn't reading off tables, putting tab A in slot B; he was living, working, and feeling the result, discovering himself growing stronger, able to do a little more and a little more. He started with only a few bricks at a time, but he kept adding them, and hauling them up the slope a little more easily each day. In an era when your exercise machine counts for nothing if it isn't computerized, this gives me a great deal of pleasure to think about.

"I believe every human heart has a finite number of beats in it. I don't intend to waste any of mine running around doing exercise."

—NEIL ARMSTRONG

MONDAY, DECEMBER 30   365

WHERE & WHEN _____ DISTANCE _____

COMMENTS _____

TUESDAY, DECEMBER 31   366

WHERE & WHEN _____ DISTANCE _____

COMMENTS _____

WEDNESDAY, JANUARY 1   1

WHERE & WHEN _____ DISTANCE _____

COMMENTS _____

THURSDAY, JANUARY 2   2

WHERE & WHEN _____ DISTANCE _____

COMMENTS _____

FRIDAY, JANUARY 3   3

WHERE & WHEN _____ DISTANCE _____

COMMENTS _____

SATURDAY, JANUARY 4

4

WHERE & WHEN —————————————————— DISTANCE ————
COMMENTS ——————————————————————————————

SUNDAY, JANUARY 5

5

WHERE & WHEN —————————————————— DISTANCE ————
COMMENTS ——————————————————————————————

In winter, one-third of the body's heat is lost through the head.

DISTANCE THIS WEEK ————————————————— WEIGHT ——————

"If other people are going to talk, conversation becomes impossible."
—JAMES McNEILL WHISTLER

MONDAY, JANUARY 6   6

WHERE & WHEN _____ DISTANCE _____
COMMENTS _____

TUESDAY, JANUARY 7   7

WHERE & WHEN _____ DISTANCE _____
COMMENTS _____

WEDNESDAY, JANUARY 8   8

WHERE & WHEN _____ DISTANCE _____
COMMENTS _____

THURSDAY, JANUARY 9   9

WHERE & WHEN _____ DISTANCE _____
COMMENTS _____

FRIDAY, JANUARY 10   10

WHERE & WHEN _____ DISTANCE _____
COMMENTS _____

WHERE & WHEN _____ DISTANCE _____
COMMENTS _____

SUNDAY, JANUARY 12   12

WHERE & WHEN _____ DISTANCE _____
COMMENTS _____

Join the intelligent minority: only 22 percent of Americans over
eighteen exercise enough to gain health benefits.

DISTANCE THIS WEEK _____ WEIGHT _____

"Having a family is like having a bowling alley installed in your brain."
—MARTIN MULL

MONDAY, JANUARY 13　　　　　　　　　　　　13

WHERE & WHEN _____ DISTANCE _____
COMMENTS _____

TUESDAY, JANUARY 14　　　　　　　　　　　　14

WHERE & WHEN _____ DISTANCE _____
COMMENTS _____

WEDNESDAY, JANUARY 15　　　　　　　　　　　15

WHERE & WHEN _____ DISTANCE _____
COMMENTS _____

THURSDAY, JANUARY 16　　　　　　　　　　　16

WHERE & WHEN _____ DISTANCE _____
COMMENTS _____

FRIDAY, JANUARY 17　　　　　　　　　　　　17

WHERE & WHEN _____ DISTANCE _____
COMMENTS _____

SATURDAY, JANUARY 18   18

_____
_____
_____
_____

WHERE & WHEN _____ DISTANCE _____
COMMENTS _____

SUNDAY, JANUARY 19   19

_____
_____
_____
_____

WHERE & WHEN _____ DISTANCE _____
COMMENTS _____

Never, ever, run on railroad tracks. It's illegal, the footing is terrible (and leads to injury), and every year about five hundred trespassers get killed there.

"Anybody can do any amount of work, provided it isn't the work he's supposed to be doing at the moment."
—ROBERT BENCHLEY

MONDAY, JANUARY 20 — 20

WHERE & WHEN _____ DISTANCE _____
COMMENTS _____

TUESDAY, JANUARY 21 — 21

WHERE & WHEN _____ DISTANCE _____
COMMENTS _____

WEDNESDAY, JANUARY 22 — 22

WHERE & WHEN _____ DISTANCE _____
COMMENTS _____

THURSDAY, JANUARY 23 — 23

WHERE & WHEN _____ DISTANCE _____
COMMENTS _____

FRIDAY, JANUARY 24 — 24

WHERE & WHEN _____ DISTANCE _____
COMMENTS _____

SATURDAY, JANUARY 25

25

WHERE & WHEN _____ DISTANCE _____

COMMENTS _____

SUNDAY, JANUARY 26

26

WHERE & WHEN _____ DISTANCE _____

COMMENTS _____

Hypertensives, hit the road: regular exercise can lower blood
pressure without medication.

DISTANCE THIS WEEK _____ WEIGHT _____

"Santa Claus has the right idea: visit people once a year."

—VICTOR BORGE

MONDAY, JANUARY 27   27

WHERE & WHEN _____ DISTANCE _____
COMMENTS _____

TUESDAY, JANUARY 28   28

WHERE & WHEN _____ DISTANCE _____
COMMENTS _____

WEDNESDAY, JANUARY 29   29

WHERE & WHEN _____ DISTANCE _____
COMMENTS _____

THURSDAY, JANUARY 30   30

WHERE & WHEN _____ DISTANCE _____
COMMENTS _____

FRIDAY, JANUARY 31   31

WHERE & WHEN _____ DISTANCE _____
COMMENTS _____

WHERE & WHEN _____ DISTANCE _____
COMMENTS _____

WHERE & WHEN _____ DISTANCE _____
COMMENTS _____

On bad footing—including ice—shorten your stride.

FEBRUARY

S	M	T	W	T	F	S
						1
2	3	4	5	6	7	8
9	10	11	12 ASH WEDNESDAY LINCOLN'S BIRTHDAY	13	14 VALENTINE'S DAY	15
16	17 PRESIDENTS' DAY	18	19	20	21	22 WASHINGTON'S BIRTHDAY
23	24	25	26	27	28	

Cold weather makes for good running, temperature-wise. I don't exactly *prefer* winter to summer, but I'd rather draw deep lungfuls of refreshment than suck in that sodden summer stuff that's already heated almost to body temperature. Running in the cold is sometimes even worth the price of wearing the extra clothing.

But we're having an open winter, with no snow to speak of, which lures me into running off the pavement, where frost has cobblestoned the ground beneath the dead grass. The footing is unpredictable, even dangerous. High-tops are called for, so you can lean the ankle against leather rather than unsupported ligaments. I don't own high-topped running shoes, however, and since it will probably snow soon anyway, forcing me back on the pavement, I think I'll pass on the investment. Of course I could always tape my ankles, as any serious athlete does in the face of risk, but isn't running supposed to be simpler than that?

The concept of ankle support reminds me of the leather wristbands that movie star Gilbert Roland used to wear. As a kid I couldn't grow one of those thin black moustaches—or smoke those thin black cigars—so I pined instead for my own leather wristband. I finally got one, and wore it even in the sweaty summers of Houston. An older kid—no doubt jealous—pointed out that it was making my wrist not stronger but actually weaker, since I was relying on the support. In fact, I couldn't tell any difference between wearing it and not wearing it; I just thought it looked cool. But my bossy friend's warning gnawed in the back of my mind: I *had* thought it would make my wrist stronger. Didn't it help Roland hold his own in all those swordfights?

In those days people were always puncturing my myths about fitness. I argued for the tallest gear I could fit on my old single-speed bike, because a tall gear made you push harder on the pedals, and that surely had to make your legs stronger. Friends insisted it was the repetitions and not the force that did the good. (Weight lifters still debate this conundrum.) I opted for the lightest available weight of "tennis shoe"—as we called sneakers in those pre-running-shoe days—on the theory that you could run faster and jump higher with less weight on your feet; my spoilsport buddies preferred the early-day equivalent of combat boots, which made them feel helium-assisted when they finally took them off. We fell for any half-baked notion about fitness that came down the pike; we didn't know anything, and therefore believed everything. Check any comic book: Charles Atlas was making a killing on people like us.

It is startling to contrast that level of gullibility with our current era of information overload. You hear people talking about VO_2 max at cocktail parties, bringing water bottles along even to go shopping—loaded, I suppose, with electrolytic replacement fluids. Nowadays everyone is an exercise physiologist.

Yet the off-hour television listings are still full of thirty-minute commercial programs for exercise gizmos. Who would possibly be watching these shows but the couch-potato, stay-indoors losers of the world? Weird, but I guess the advertisers know their markets. Maybe I'll bring out a line of leather wristbands.

"The great ones always keep it simple."

—JACK WHITTAKER

MONDAY, FEBRUARY 3   34

WHERE & WHEN _____ DISTANCE _____
COMMENTS _____

TUESDAY, FEBRUARY 4   35

WHERE & WHEN _____ DISTANCE _____
COMMENTS _____

WEDNESDAY, FEBRUARY 5   36

WHERE & WHEN _____ DISTANCE _____
COMMENTS _____

THURSDAY, FEBRUARY 6   37

WHERE & WHEN _____ DISTANCE _____
COMMENTS _____

FRIDAY, FEBRUARY 7   38

WHERE & WHEN _____ DISTANCE _____
COMMENTS _____

WHERE & WHEN _____ DISTANCE _____

COMMENTS _____

WHERE & WHEN _____ DISTANCE _____

COMMENTS _____

If your running is not satisfying to you, you're probably running
too fast, too far, or too often.

"Why shouldn't things be largely absurd, futile, and transitory? They are so, and we are so, and they and we go well together."

—GEORGE SANTAYANA

MONDAY, FEBRUARY 10   41

WHERE & WHEN _____ DISTANCE _____
COMMENTS _____

TUESDAY, FEBRUARY 11   42

WHERE & WHEN _____ DISTANCE _____
COMMENTS _____

WEDNESDAY, FEBRUARY 12   43

WHERE & WHEN _____ DISTANCE _____
COMMENTS _____

THURSDAY, FEBRUARY 13   44

WHERE & WHEN _____ DISTANCE _____
COMMENTS _____

FRIDAY, FEBRUARY 14   45

WHERE & WHEN _____ DISTANCE _____
COMMENTS _____

SATURDAY, FEBRUARY 15

WHERE & WHEN _____ DISTANCE _____
COMMENTS _____

SUNDAY, FEBRUARY 16

WHERE & WHEN _____ DISTANCE _____
COMMENTS _____

Training at altitude improves your performance at altitude. To
improve at sea level you have to train at sea level.

DISTANCE THIS WEEK _____ WEIGHT _____

"A man gazing at the stars is proverbially at the mercy of the puddles in the road."
　　　　　　　　　　　　　　　　　　　　　　　—ALEXANDER SMITH

MONDAY, FEBRUARY 17　　　　　　　　　　　　　48

WHERE & WHEN _____ DISTANCE _____
COMMENTS _____

TUESDAY, FEBRUARY 18　　　　　　　　　　　　49

WHERE & WHEN _____ DISTANCE _____
COMMENTS _____

WEDNESDAY, FEBRUARY 19　　　　　　　　　　　50

WHERE & WHEN _____ DISTANCE _____
COMMENTS _____

THURSDAY, FEBRUARY 20　　　　　　　　　　　51

WHERE & WHEN _____ DISTANCE _____
COMMENTS _____

FRIDAY, FEBRUARY 21　　　　　　　　　　　　52

WHERE & WHEN _____ DISTANCE _____
COMMENTS _____

WHERE & WHEN ——————————————— DISTANCE ————
COMMENTS ————————————————————————

WHERE & WHEN ——————————————— DISTANCE ————
COMMENTS ————————————————————————

Your body language, if under control, can tell your competitors
that they're already beaten.

DISTANCE THIS WEEK ————————————— WEIGHT ————

"I took a speed reading course and read War and Peace *in twenty minutes. It involves Russia."*
—WOODY ALLEN

MONDAY, FEBRUARY 24   55

_____
_____
_____
_____

WHERE & WHEN _____ DISTANCE _____
COMMENTS _____
_____

TUESDAY, FEBRUARY 25   56

_____
_____
_____
_____

WHERE & WHEN _____ DISTANCE _____
COMMENTS _____
_____

WEDNESDAY, FEBRUARY 26   57

_____
_____
_____
_____

WHERE & WHEN _____ DISTANCE _____
COMMENTS _____
_____

THURSDAY, FEBRUARY 27   58

_____
_____
_____
_____

WHERE & WHEN _____ DISTANCE _____
COMMENTS _____
_____

FRIDAY, FEBRUARY 28   59

_____
_____
_____
_____

WHERE & WHEN _____ DISTANCE _____
COMMENTS _____
_____

WHERE & WHEN _____ DISTANCE _____

COMMENTS _____

WHERE & WHEN _____ DISTANCE _____

COMMENTS _____

Respect the wind: dress in layers, stay as dry as possible,
drink liquids.

DISTANCE THIS WEEK _____ WEIGHT _____

MARCH

S	M	T	W	T	F	S
						1
2	3	4	5	6	7	8
9	10	11	12	13	14	15
16	17 ST. PATRICK'S DAY	18	19	20	21	22
23 PALM SUNDAY	24	25	26	27	28 GOOD FRIDAY	29
30 EASTER	31					

March: Madness

The annual college basketball national championships are upon us, filling the home screen with exuberant young athleticism. TV calls this period "March Madness," a term that carries the image of craziness, March hares, loony bursts of springtime energies. In my neck of the woods, it's much too early for that. Hereabouts the sweet part of spring, when every day the woods in particular become a more delicious place in which to run, is still a few weeks away.

The basketball championships aren't about springtime anyway; they're about grinding the other team down. The tournament is a long, exhausting process, and the team that wins is usually the one that either somehow miraculously avoids injuries to key players, or that has a deep bench. Coaches delight in "putting some hurt" on the opposition, and other athletic clichés. They watch for every telltale sign of weakness, for pressure points. If you catch your opponents hanging on their shorts at the free-throw line, you immediately call for a full-court press. You've got their tongues hanging out; now run 'em ragged.

I have a problem with this aspect of competition, very likely a hangover from the Boy Scouts or some other Victorian institution. When I was competing regularly, what I wanted to do—perhaps too idealistically—was to win on the basis of my own energies and skills. When psychology entered into it, something a little poisonous came into the contest. I always felt that trying to psych people out, looking for an edge, searching for ways to make it more painful for the other fellow, took a little of the fun out of it. When your opponent is no longer capable of full response, it stops being a contest. "Take your best shot" is far from an empty challenge: it is exactly what you want the other fellow to do, just as it's what you want to do yourself.

Athletics doesn't have to be this way, of course. Your competitors, after all, are joined with you in an enterprise aimed at bringing out the best in you as well as themselves. Looked at in those terms, it is possible—in fact not even unusual—to be swept with a feeling for one's adversaries, the moment the finish line is crossed, that's pretty close to love.

I've certainly had that feeling myself, which is perhaps why something about the adversary stage bothers me. When I see my competitor begin to fade, I feel a little surge of selfish joy. Can't help it. But I don't like it; it is not ennobling; it is tainted, somehow, corrupting.

This reaction has to do with me, not with the competition or the sport. I'm not proud of it or moralistic about it, except perhaps to myself. Competition lights a little fire in me that I would prefer not to have lit. It is rather like the impulse to steal or to be unfaithful. It is an occasion of sin. It makes me uneasy.

There is a problem, however, with this attempt at nobility. That psychology stuff can work two ways. I notice that the moment one begins embracing one's competitors, on some level one starts settling for second place. I like coming in second even less than I like seeing the other fellow drop out. Conundrums like this can drive you a little crazy along about March.

"The optimist thinks that this is the best of all possible worlds, and the pessimist knows it."
—J. ROBERT OPPENHEIMER

MONDAY, MARCH 3   62

WHERE & WHEN _____ DISTANCE _____
COMMENTS _____

TUESDAY, MARCH 4   63

WHERE & WHEN _____ DISTANCE _____
COMMENTS _____

WEDNESDAY, MARCH 5   64

WHERE & WHEN _____ DISTANCE _____
COMMENTS _____

THURSDAY, MARCH 6   65

WHERE & WHEN _____ DISTANCE _____
COMMENTS _____

FRIDAY, MARCH 7   66

WHERE & WHEN _____ DISTANCE _____
COMMENTS _____

WHERE & WHEN _____ DISTANCE _____
COMMENTS _____

SUNDAY, MARCH 9   68

WHERE & WHEN _____ DISTANCE _____
COMMENTS _____

It *is* a beer belly: alcohol slows down the burning of fat, and
unburned fat is stored you-know-where, at least in men. In women
it's more likely to go to the thighs.

"Lead me not into temptation. I can find the way myself."

—RITA MAE BROWN

MONDAY, MARCH 10   69

WHERE & WHEN _____ DISTANCE _____
COMMENTS _____

TUESDAY, MARCH 11   70

WHERE & WHEN _____ DISTANCE _____
COMMENTS _____

WEDNESDAY, MARCH 12   71

WHERE & WHEN _____ DISTANCE _____
COMMENTS _____

THURSDAY, MARCH 13   72

WHERE & WHEN _____ DISTANCE _____
COMMENTS _____

FRIDAY, MARCH 14   73

WHERE & WHEN _____ DISTANCE _____
COMMENTS _____

SATURDAY, MARCH 15   74

WHERE & WHEN _____ DISTANCE _____
COMMENTS _____

SUNDAY, MARCH 16   75

WHERE & WHEN _____ DISTANCE _____
COMMENTS _____

DISTANCE THIS WEEK _____ WEIGHT _____

"The first half of our life is ruined by our parents and the second half by our children."
——CLARENCE DARROW

MONDAY, MARCH 17   76

WHERE & WHEN _____ DISTANCE _____
COMMENTS _____

TUESDAY, MARCH 18   77

WHERE & WHEN _____ DISTANCE _____
COMMENTS _____

WEDNESDAY, MARCH 19   78

WHERE & WHEN _____ DISTANCE _____
COMMENTS _____

THURSDAY, MARCH 20   79

WHERE & WHEN _____ DISTANCE _____
COMMENTS _____

FRIDAY, MARCH 21   80

WHERE & WHEN _____ DISTANCE _____
COMMENTS _____

WHERE & WHEN _____ DISTANCE _____
COMMENTS _____

WHERE & WHEN _____ DISTANCE _____
COMMENTS _____

Carbon monoxide levels can be twice as high on tree-lined streets,
where automobile emissions are sometimes trapped.

DISTANCE THIS WEEK _____ WEIGHT _____

"Every normal man must be tempted at times to spit on his hands, hoist the black flag, and begin slitting throats."
—H. L. MENCKEN

MONDAY, MARCH 24   83

WHERE & WHEN _____ DISTANCE _____
COMMENTS _____

TUESDAY, MARCH 25   84

WHERE & WHEN _____ DISTANCE _____
COMMENTS _____

WEDNESDAY, MARCH 26   85

WHERE & WHEN _____ DISTANCE _____
COMMENTS _____

THURSDAY, MARCH 27   86

WHERE & WHEN _____ DISTANCE _____
COMMENTS _____

FRIDAY, MARCH 28   87

WHERE & WHEN _____ DISTANCE _____
COMMENTS _____

SATURDAY, MARCH 29

WHERE & WHEN _____ DISTANCE _____

COMMENTS _____

_____

SUNDAY, MARCH 30

WHERE & WHEN _____ DISTANCE _____

COMMENTS _____

_____

Midsoles of running shoes break down before the outer soles
show wear.

DISTANCE THIS WEEK _____ WEIGHT _____

APRIL

S	M	T	W	T	F	S
		1	2	3	4	5
6	7	8	9	10	11	12
13	14	15	16	17	18	19
20	21	22	23	24	25	26
27	28	29 PASSOVER	30			

April: Earth-Grabbing Activities

An early-morning errand requires that I use my car (and postpone running past my favorite time of day). I pass a young woman striding purposefully along, obviously walking for fitness. Within a few minutes I see two more. Then, in amusing contrast, I see an old guy just sauntering along, inspecting the roadside ditch. Strolling. The difference makes me smile. It is striking, almost as dramatic as the difference between running and walking. Attitude is everything.

Like many runners I was mildly entertained a few years back by fad-mongers who made a big deal out of walking. You know, walking shoes, walking gear, walking magazines, walking clubs and organizations, walking tours and other travel promotions: ways to sell natural human locomotion as a new discovery.

Not that walking isn't a terrific activity. Far be it from me to go fomenting disagreement, dividing yet another segment of our society into *them* vs. *us*. I enjoy walking myself, particularly when I've gone orthopedic and need to keep moving while I heal. After all, movement—and its pleasures—are what we're all about, and however you want to achieve it is your own affair. Ask me along and I'll join you. Or you might prefer to do it alone, a perfectly understandable proclivity. Both walking and running encourage a reflective approach to life, which I figure is a net gain, and reflection is usually more fruitful when practiced solo.

Actually, to separate walking from running is to establish a distinction that doesn't exist, or shouldn't. Whether we run or walk, we do it by reaching out with our legs and grabbing terrain—or distance—and passing that terrain under us. Pushing off from it, grabbing for more. These are earth-grabbing activities. Some walkers might claim that a run is for the body and a walk is for the soul— see attitude, above—but we should all recognize that either works for both.

My all-time favorite reflective person is Henry David Thoreau. He wasn't much of a runner—he sent someone else for help once, when he set the woods on fire— but he was a great walker, four hours a day, rain or shine, sometimes walking through the night. His journal entry for February 12, 1851, could be addressed to runners as well, and reflects a curious light on our modern-day situation as runners: "I trust that the walkers of the present day are conscious of the blessings which they enjoy in the comparative freedom with which they can ramble over the country and enjoy the landscape, anticipating with compassion that future day when possibly it will be partitioned off into so-called pleasure-grounds, where only a few may enjoy the narrow and exclusive pleasure which is compatible with ownership,—when walking over the surface of God's earth shall be construed to mean trespassing on some gentleman's grounds, when fences shall be multiplied and man traps and other engines invented to confine men to the public road. I am thankful that we have yet so much room in America."

Old Henry seemed already to be worried, nearly a hundred and fifty years ago, about another sort of earth-grabbing activity. I think he'd be surprised at how much walking—and running—room we've managed to preserve for our personal pleasures. I believe I'll go for a run and think about this. Maybe I'll walk home.

"No man has ever admitted that he is rich—or that he was asleep when you called."

—PATRICK O'BRIAN

MONDAY, MARCH 31   90

WHERE & WHEN _____ DISTANCE _____
COMMENTS _____

TUESDAY, APRIL 1   91

WHERE & WHEN _____ DISTANCE _____
COMMENTS _____

WEDNESDAY, APRIL 2   92

WHERE & WHEN _____ DISTANCE _____
COMMENTS _____

THURSDAY, APRIL 3   93

WHERE & WHEN _____ DISTANCE _____
COMMENTS _____

FRIDAY, APRIL 4   94

WHERE & WHEN _____ DISTANCE _____
COMMENTS _____

WHERE & WHEN ———————————————— DISTANCE ————
COMMENTS ————————————————————————————————

WHERE & WHEN ———————————————— DISTANCE ————
COMMENTS ————————————————————————————————

You need 2 percent fewer calories every decade.

"Brevity is the soul of lingerie."

—DOROTHY PARKER

MONDAY, APRIL 7   97

WHERE & WHEN _____ DISTANCE _____
COMMENTS _____

TUESDAY, APRIL 8   98

WHERE & WHEN _____ DISTANCE _____
COMMENTS _____

WEDNESDAY, APRIL 9   99

WHERE & WHEN _____ DISTANCE _____
COMMENTS _____

THURSDAY, APRIL 10   100

WHERE & WHEN _____ DISTANCE _____
COMMENTS _____

FRIDAY, APRIL 11   101

WHERE & WHEN _____ DISTANCE _____
COMMENTS _____

WHERE & WHEN _____ DISTANCE _____

COMMENTS _____

WHERE & WHEN _____ DISTANCE _____

COMMENTS _____

Take a short break between warm-up and work-out: your work-out
will go better if you start on a wave of recovery.

DISTANCE THIS WEEK _____ WEIGHT _____

"If you stay in Beverly Hills too long you become a Mercedes-Benz."

—ROBERT REDFORD

MONDAY, APRIL 14   104

WHERE & WHEN _____ DISTANCE _____
COMMENTS _____

TUESDAY, APRIL 15   105

WHERE & WHEN _____ DISTANCE _____
COMMENTS _____

WEDNESDAY, APRIL 16   106

WHERE & WHEN _____ DISTANCE _____
COMMENTS _____

THURSDAY, APRIL 17   107

WHERE & WHEN _____ DISTANCE _____
COMMENTS _____

FRIDAY, APRIL 18   108

WHERE & WHEN _____ DISTANCE _____
COMMENTS _____

WHERE & WHEN _____ DISTANCE _____

COMMENTS _____

WHERE & WHEN _____ DISTANCE _____

COMMENTS _____

If summer running gives you a headache, watery eyes, tightness of the chest, a runny nose, or uncomfortably dry nasal passages, the problem is probably air pollution.

"Nature is always hinting at us. It hints over and over again. And suddenly we take the hint."
—ROBERT FROST

MONDAY, APRIL 21   111

WHERE & WHEN _____ DISTANCE _____
COMMENTS _____

TUESDAY, APRIL 22   112

WHERE & WHEN _____ DISTANCE _____
COMMENTS _____

WEDNESDAY, APRIL 23   113

WHERE & WHEN _____ DISTANCE _____
COMMENTS _____

THURSDAY, APRIL 24   114

WHERE & WHEN _____ DISTANCE _____
COMMENTS _____

FRIDAY, APRIL 25   115

WHERE & WHEN _____ DISTANCE _____
COMMENTS _____

WHERE & WHEN _____ DISTANCE _____

COMMENTS _____

WHERE & WHEN _____ DISTANCE _____

COMMENTS _____

Sometimes we forget: injuring yourself *hurts*.

DISTANCE THIS WEEK _____ WEIGHT _____

"Nothing is so aggravating as calmness."

—OSCAR WILDE

MONDAY, APRIL 28   118

WHERE & WHEN _____ DISTANCE _____
COMMENTS _____

TUESDAY, APRIL 29   119

WHERE & WHEN _____ DISTANCE _____
COMMENTS _____

WEDNESDAY, APRIL 30   120

WHERE & WHEN _____ DISTANCE _____
COMMENTS _____

THURSDAY, MAY 1   121

WHERE & WHEN _____ DISTANCE _____
COMMENTS _____

FRIDAY, MAY 2   122

WHERE & WHEN _____ DISTANCE _____
COMMENTS _____

WHERE & WHEN _____ DISTANCE _____

COMMENTS _____

WHERE & WHEN _____ DISTANCE _____

COMMENTS _____

MAY

S	M	T	W	T	F	S
				1	2	3
4	5	6	7	8	9	10
11 MOTHER'S DAY	12	13	14	15	16	17
18	19 VICTORIA DAY (CANADA)	20	21	22	23	24
25	26 MEMORIAL DAY OBSERVED	27	28	29	30	31 MEMORIAL DAY

May: On the Verge

Sunday, the first week of May: I'd planned on doing yardwork, but it's too cold, springtime on hold, windy enough to knock you down out there. I'll wait for a nicer day.

Ah, but my favorite woods trail is fairly sheltered, so I decide to go for a run instead. Unfortunately my mood as I start out is not a good one. I am decidedly unambitious, determined to do nothing more than work my muscles and lungs. Move my blood, clean the system out a bit; that's all I'm after, I swear it. And sure enough, until I get heart and respiration up to speed, that is goal enough. It takes up most of my attention: an interesting process when you focus on it.

When that focus fades—when I get my head out of my own physiology—my mind wanders off into the usual junk, all those exigencies of everyday life: money, health, family, career. The anxieties of the future, the regrets of the past—not very fruitful things to think about, but unavoidable somehow. The next time I fill out an application I plan to list my occupation as "Worry."

It is a strange day: hard frost last night, brilliant dawn, at noon the blustery cold front buffeting me, the wind roaring in the treetops even at those rare times when it isn't impeding my progress here on ground level. The branches over-head are still bare, giving the wind less to hang on to. There's also not much to filter the strong May sun that comes pouring down. There's little shade in the woods, which is strange enough, and the light is exceedingly white, wintry, with nothing to bounce off of but bare gray trees and the beige leaf mold of the forest floor. Six months ago that duff was riotously orange and red, making a run in these woods a trip down a glowing chromatic tunnel; now it's almost stark—out of place, out of season, for a New England forest. (It's so dazzling it reminds me of the quality of light that filmmakers use to make fun of L.A.)

Trilliums are beginning to peek through the duff. The understory is trying to pop, three-dimensional polka-dots under what will eventually be full canopy. You can still see a good distance through the woods, as you can in deep winter; in another three weeks you'll no longer be able to do that. Hemlocks provide what little shade there is, and that shade is bluer somehow, cooler than usual. At the edge of the shade the white light is blinding. My maximum visual range is about fifty yards; in three weeks that circle will be cut to twenty.

How odd it is, a human organism moving through the woods carrying a fifty-yard circle of visual range ahead of it. Of course I also carry along a much larger circle of hearing, and a much smaller circle of smell. Two circles of smell, actu-ally, the incoming and the outgoing.

Oh my gosh, look what's happened: I went off there and did all that work just for my body and didn't even notice. I also forgot to spend any worrying time on all that regrettable-past and anxiety-filled-future business. I just went out the door and ventured for a small distance across the surface of the earth, and enjoyed every moment of it. Enjoyed thinking that; enjoyed being on the planet.

Gee, my mood seems to have changed.

"One of the delights known to age, and beyond the grasp of youth, is that of Not Going."
—J. B. PRIESTLY

MONDAY, MAY 5   125

WHERE & WHEN _____ DISTANCE _____
COMMENTS _____

TUESDAY, MAY 6   126

WHERE & WHEN _____ DISTANCE _____
COMMENTS _____

WEDNESDAY, MAY 7   127

WHERE & WHEN _____ DISTANCE _____
COMMENTS _____

THURSDAY, MAY 8   128

WHERE & WHEN _____ DISTANCE _____
COMMENTS _____

FRIDAY, MAY 9   129

WHERE & WHEN _____ DISTANCE _____
COMMENTS _____

WHERE & WHEN _____ DISTANCE _____
COMMENTS _____

WHERE & WHEN _____ DISTANCE _____
COMMENTS _____

A week of complete bed rest ages your body by about ten years.
Fortunately, exercise de-ages it right back again.

"Few things are harder to put up with than the annoyance of a good example."
                                                                    —MARK TWAIN

MONDAY, MAY 12   132

WHERE & WHEN _____ DISTANCE _____
COMMENTS _____

TUESDAY, MAY 13   133

WHERE & WHEN _____ DISTANCE _____
COMMENTS _____

WEDNESDAY, MAY 14   134

WHERE & WHEN _____ DISTANCE _____
COMMENTS _____

THURSDAY, MAY 15   135

WHERE & WHEN _____ DISTANCE _____
COMMENTS _____

FRIDAY, MAY 16   136

WHERE & WHEN _____ DISTANCE _____
COMMENTS _____

WHERE & WHEN _____ DISTANCE _____

COMMENTS _____

WHERE & WHEN _____ DISTANCE _____

COMMENTS _____

"Today, communication itself is the problem. We have become the world's first over-communicated society. Each year we send more and receive less."
—AL RIES

MONDAY, MAY 19　　　　139

WHERE & WHEN _____ DISTANCE _____
COMMENTS _____

TUESDAY, MAY 20　　　　140

WHERE & WHEN _____ DISTANCE _____
COMMENTS _____

WEDNESDAY, MAY 21　　　　141

WHERE & WHEN _____ DISTANCE _____
COMMENTS _____

THURSDAY, MAY 22　　　　142

WHERE & WHEN _____ DISTANCE _____
COMMENTS _____

FRIDAY, MAY 23　　　　143

WHERE & WHEN _____ DISTANCE _____
COMMENTS _____

WHERE & WHEN _____ DISTANCE _____
COMMENTS _____

WHERE & WHEN _____ DISTANCE _____
COMMENTS _____

Chill out: in tests on stationary bikes, remembered anger decreased
pedaling efficiency by 5 percent.

"Virtue is insufficient temptation." —GEORGE BERNARD SHAW

MONDAY, MAY 26 146

WHERE & WHEN _____ DISTANCE _____
COMMENTS _____

TUESDAY, MAY 27 147

WHERE & WHEN _____ DISTANCE _____
COMMENTS _____

WEDNESDAY, MAY 28 148

WHERE & WHEN _____ DISTANCE _____
COMMENTS _____

THURSDAY, MAY 29 149

WHERE & WHEN _____ DISTANCE _____
COMMENTS _____

FRIDAY, MAY 30 150

WHERE & WHEN _____ DISTANCE _____
COMMENTS _____

WHERE & WHEN _____ DISTANCE _____

COMMENTS _____

WHERE & WHEN _____ DISTANCE _____

COMMENTS _____

DISTANCE THIS WEEK _____ WEIGHT _____

JUNE

S	M	T	W	T	F	S
1	2	3	4	5	6	7
8	9	10	11	12	13	14
15 FATHER'S DAY	16	17	18	19	20	21
22	23	24	25	26	27	28
29	30					

One of the unexpected dividends in writing this *Log* for the past twelve years has been a relationship that has built up with reader-runners. Something I've said will strike a spark—sometimes a fiery one—and the reader will write to Random House with a personal message, which eventually finds its way to me.

One particularly pointed letter had to do with a photograph of two runners who chose to run in the middle of the road on a blind curve. Why, he wanted to know, would we show such a dangerous practice? Good point. Since that time we've tried hard to exclude the truly stupid from our pages, but we failed to catch another, similar photograph, this time of some idiot running on a railroad track. That brought the largest flurry of letters, a lot of them from railroad workers who were also runners. Trespassing on railroad right-of-ways is not only illegal, they pointed out, but extremely dangerous: some 500 people are killed there every year. We were terribly embarrassed at that goof, and every year since have included a warning against this practice in the tips that accompany the text.

Some fairly lengthy correspondences have developed. One of the most useful has been with Tom Newcomb, of Olympia, Washington. We've had a continuing dialogue with Tom over various features of the *Log*, and he's come up with some very good suggestions. "While it may seem silly to elite runners," Tom says, "we slower runners can be meticulous at recording our splits. We aren't running against them, but rather against ourselves. You don't have to be 'good' to be a runner! "Someday I suppose they'll invent a watch that does all this for you. I bought my watch 'cause it can record thirty separate laps. I usually wait until I have a few left before going to my *Log* and entering the data. Sometimes it takes some real thinking to remember which way I ran on the first one." Tom points out that when you regularly do arithmetic with minutes and seconds—as in dividing miles into lap times—you quickly discover the need to convert seconds to a decimal equivalent and then back to seconds again. He's worked out the following handy conversion chart for that process:

TOM NEWCOMB'S SECOND-TO-DECIMAL CONVERSION CHART

SEC	DEC	SEC	DEC	SEC	DEC	SEC	DEC	SEC	DEC	SEC	DEC
00	.0000	10	.1666	20	.3333	30	.5000	40	.6666	50	.8333
01	.0166	11	.1833	21	.3500	31	.5166	41	.6833	51	.8500
02	.0333	12	.2000	22	.3666	32	.5333	42	.7000	52	.8666
03	.0500	13	.2166	23	.3833	33	.5500	43	.7166	53	.8833
04	.0666	14	.2333	24	.4000	34	.5666	44	.7333	54	.9000
05	.0833	15	.2500	25	.4166	35	.5833	45	.7500	55	.9166
06	.1000	16	.2666	26	.4333	36	.6000	46	.7666	56	.9333
07	.1166	17	.2833	27	.4500	37	.6166	47	.7833	57	.9500
08	.1333	18	.3000	28	.4666	38	.6333	48	.8000	58	.9666
09	.1500	19	.3166	29	.4833	39	.6500	49	.8166	59	.9833

"There was no one in the vicinity to confuse and annoy me, and so I had to be original."

—JOSEPH HAYDN

MONDAY, JUNE 2   153

WHERE & WHEN _____ DISTANCE _____
COMMENTS _____

TUESDAY, JUNE 3   154

WHERE & WHEN _____ DISTANCE _____
COMMENTS _____

WEDNESDAY, JUNE 4   155

WHERE & WHEN _____ DISTANCE _____
COMMENTS _____

THURSDAY, JUNE 5   156

WHERE & WHEN _____ DISTANCE _____
COMMENTS _____

FRIDAY, JUNE 6   157

WHERE & WHEN _____ DISTANCE _____
COMMENTS _____

SATURDAY, JUNE 7

WHERE & WHEN ———————————————— DISTANCE ————
COMMENTS ——————————————————————————

SUNDAY, JUNE 8

WHERE & WHEN ———————————————— DISTANCE ————
COMMENTS ——————————————————————————

If you're temporarily on medication, you probably shouldn't
be running.

DISTANCE THIS WEEK ————————————— WEIGHT ——————

"Everything considered, work is less boring than amusing oneself."
—BAUDELAIRE

MONDAY, JUNE 9 160

WHERE & WHEN _____ DISTANCE _____
COMMENTS _____

TUESDAY, JUNE 10 161

WHERE & WHEN _____ DISTANCE _____
COMMENTS _____

WEDNESDAY, JUNE 11 162

WHERE & WHEN _____ DISTANCE _____
COMMENTS _____

THURSDAY, JUNE 12 163

WHERE & WHEN _____ DISTANCE _____
COMMENTS _____

FRIDAY, JUNE 13 164

WHERE & WHEN _____ DISTANCE _____
COMMENTS _____

WHERE & WHEN _____ DISTANCE _____
COMMENTS _____

WHERE & WHEN _____ DISTANCE _____
COMMENTS _____

If you're running in a strange place, choose a simple out-and-back
course to prevent getting lost.

DISTANCE THIS WEEK _____ WEIGHT _____

"Suburbia is where the developer bulldozes out the trees, then names the streets after them."
—BILL VAUGHN

MONDAY, JUNE 16   167

WHERE & WHEN _____ DISTANCE _____
COMMENTS _____

TUESDAY, JUNE 17   168

WHERE & WHEN _____ DISTANCE _____
COMMENTS _____

WEDNESDAY, JUNE 18   169

WHERE & WHEN _____ DISTANCE _____
COMMENTS _____

THURSDAY, JUNE 19   170

WHERE & WHEN _____ DISTANCE _____
COMMENTS _____

FRIDAY, JUNE 20   171

WHERE & WHEN _____ DISTANCE _____
COMMENTS _____

SATURDAY, JUNE 21

WHERE & WHEN _____ DISTANCE _____
COMMENTS _____

SUNDAY, JUNE 22

WHERE & WHEN _____ DISTANCE _____
COMMENTS _____

DISTANCE THIS WEEK _____ WEIGHT _____

"The first rule of intelligent tinkering is to save all the parts."

—ALDO LEOPOLD

MONDAY, JUNE 23   174

WHERE & WHEN _____ DISTANCE _____
COMMENTS _____

TUESDAY, JUNE 24   175

WHERE & WHEN _____ DISTANCE _____
COMMENTS _____

WEDNESDAY, JUNE 25   176

WHERE & WHEN _____ DISTANCE _____
COMMENTS _____

THURSDAY, JUNE 26   177

WHERE & WHEN _____ DISTANCE _____
COMMENTS _____

FRIDAY, JUNE 27   178

WHERE & WHEN _____ DISTANCE _____
COMMENTS _____

WHERE & WHEN _____ DISTANCE _____
COMMENTS _____

WHERE & WHEN _____ DISTANCE _____
COMMENTS _____

Vitamins E and C may help protect against air pollution.

DISTANCE THIS WEEK _____ WEIGHT _____

JULY

S	M	T	W	T	F	S
		1 CANADA DAY	2	3	4 INDEPENDENCE DAY	5
6	7	8	9	10	11	12
13	14	15	16	17	18	19
20	21	22	23	24	25	26
27	28	29	30	31		

July: Tree Swallows, Kids, Summer Lawns

We are in deep summer now, the season when tree swallows do their fanciest flying, and I sit—sedentary, I guiltily admit—watching them, marveling at the pure physical glory of the sight. When they're not skimming our pond to snatch bugs off the surface, they seem to spend their time in mad chase scenes, tag teams pursuing each other endlessly, like kids whirling around a playground. They can't seem to resist; one will swirl past and three others will start up out of nowhere, just to get in on the action. It's anthropomorphic of me, I realize, but they seem to be having so much fun. A solo bird will soar upward, give a double-wing lunge like the butterfly swimming stroke, kick over past the stall and dive, wings folded, making linked S-turns with its tailfeathers alone. Chasing more bugs, I suppose, but I can't resist imagining that the swallow might be giving off little birdy giggles of joy at how good it feels to zip through the air that way.

The greatest gift that running has given me—after continuing health, a daily visit to my interior life, and a warm feeling for everyone else who enjoys the sport—is what might be called a sympathy for physiology. Not in the poor-baby sense of sympathy, but in the isn't-that-wonderful sense. The training effect itself, that capacity of the physical organism to improve in response to effort, is the most delicious small piece of physiology I know. I wouldn't have learned it if I weren't a runner. The discovery, or re-discovery, of the pleasure of movement for movement's sake—which in its fidgety small-child version will drive any sane adult bananas—is an even greater gift.

Kids plus a summer evening plus a nice stretch of lawn equals the birth of gymnastics, of course. Cartwheels and pyramids, headstands and handstands; bend over and put your hands between your legs, and some tall participatory adult would grab your wrists and yank you upward into a front flip, depositing you gently on your feet; would swing you around by your arms; would sometimes even join you in twirling around, getting deliberately dizzy just to play the game of Statue. Red Rover, Red Rover, let (the smallest kid) come over.

The lawn game of choice in Ingram, Texas, was called Booger Bear in the Mush Pot—a name I've heard nowhere else. The Mush Pot was a ten-foot circle in the center of the lawn. Home bases were marked off at each end of the field. Booger Bear was a free-roving chaser who could, by pointing and counting to ten, force any player to leave the safety of home base, but then had to catch said player before he or she could dart safely to the base at the other end of the field. If Booger Bear caught chasee, chasee went into the Mush Pot, but subsequent chasees could release Mush Pot captives by tagging them as they ran by. The game continued until all were caught, and the last caught became the new Booger Bear. Played barefoot, of course.

I had never heard of Booger Bear in the Mush Pot being played anywhere else, but in my dotage I discover it is nothing but a version of Ringalevio, played with grim abandon on the streets of Brooklyn, as well as everywhere else in the East. Those poor little devils have to play it on pavement, though.

"If it weren't for the fact that the TV set and the refrigerator are so far apart, some of us wouldn't get any exercise at all." —JOEY ADAMS

MONDAY, JUNE 30   181

WHERE & WHEN _____ DISTANCE _____
COMMENTS _____

TUESDAY, JULY 1   182

WHERE & WHEN _____ DISTANCE _____
COMMENTS _____

WEDNESDAY, JULY 2   183

WHERE & WHEN _____ DISTANCE _____
COMMENTS _____

THURSDAY, JULY 3   184

WHERE & WHEN _____ DISTANCE _____
COMMENTS _____

FRIDAY, JULY 4   185

WHERE & WHEN _____ DISTANCE _____
COMMENTS _____

SATURDAY, JULY 5 186

WHERE & WHEN _____ DISTANCE _____
COMMENTS _____

SUNDAY, JULY 6 187

WHERE & WHEN _____ DISTANCE _____
COMMENTS _____

Jet lag is reduced by exercise.

DISTANCE THIS WEEK _____ WEIGHT _____

"I always keep a supply of stimulant handy in case I see a snake, which I also keep handy."
                                                                    —W. C. FIELDS

MONDAY, JULY 7   188

WHERE & WHEN _____ DISTANCE _____
COMMENTS _____

TUESDAY, JULY 8   189

WHERE & WHEN _____ DISTANCE _____
COMMENTS _____

WEDNESDAY, JULY 9   190

WHERE & WHEN _____ DISTANCE _____
COMMENTS _____

THURSDAY, JULY 10   191

WHERE & WHEN _____ DISTANCE _____
COMMENTS _____

FRIDAY, JULY 11   192

WHERE & WHEN _____ DISTANCE _____
COMMENTS _____

WHERE & WHEN _____ DISTANCE _____
COMMENTS _____

WHERE & WHEN _____ DISTANCE _____
COMMENTS _____

To get good gas mileage, hold the pedal steady on hills, letting the
car slow down on the way up and speed up on the way down. This
works equally well for runners.

"Happy people do not need festivity."   —QUENTIN CRISP

MONDAY, JULY 14   195

WHERE & WHEN _____ DISTANCE _____
COMMENTS _____
_____

TUESDAY, JULY 15   196

WHERE & WHEN _____ DISTANCE _____
COMMENTS _____
_____

WEDNESDAY, JULY 16   197

WHERE & WHEN _____ DISTANCE _____
COMMENTS _____
_____

THURSDAY, JULY 17   198

WHERE & WHEN _____ DISTANCE _____
COMMENTS _____
_____

FRIDAY, JULY 18   199

WHERE & WHEN _____ DISTANCE _____
COMMENTS _____
_____

WHERE & WHEN _____ DISTANCE _____
COMMENTS _____

WHERE & WHEN _____ DISTANCE _____
COMMENTS _____

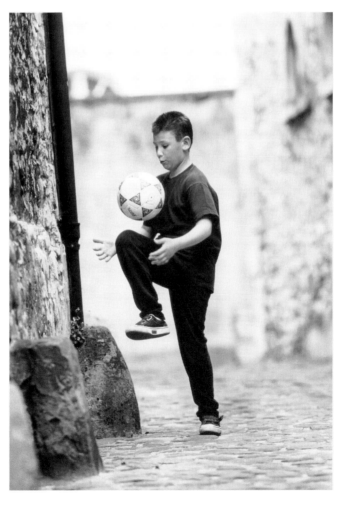

"Advertising is the rattling of a stick inside a swill bucket."

—GEORGE ORWELL

MONDAY, JULY 21   202

WHERE & WHEN _____ DISTANCE _____
COMMENTS _____

TUESDAY, JULY 22   203

WHERE & WHEN _____ DISTANCE _____
COMMENTS _____

WEDNESDAY, JULY 23   204

WHERE & WHEN _____ DISTANCE _____
COMMENTS _____

THURSDAY, JULY 24   205

WHERE & WHEN _____ DISTANCE _____
COMMENTS _____

FRIDAY, JULY 25   206

WHERE & WHEN _____ DISTANCE _____
COMMENTS _____

WHERE & WHEN _____ DISTANCE _____

COMMENTS _____

WHERE & WHEN _____ DISTANCE _____

COMMENTS _____

You never lose your ability to adapt to muscular load. Nursing-
home residents who lift weights have increased their strength
by 200 percent.

DISTANCE THIS WEEK _____ WEIGHT _____

"Marriage: a friendship recognized by the police."

—ROBERT LOUIS STEVENSON

MONDAY, JULY 28   209

WHERE & WHEN _____ DISTANCE _____
COMMENTS _____

TUESDAY, JULY 29   210

WHERE & WHEN _____ DISTANCE _____
COMMENTS _____

WEDNESDAY, JULY 30   211

WHERE & WHEN _____ DISTANCE _____
COMMENTS _____

THURSDAY, JULY 31   212

WHERE & WHEN _____ DISTANCE _____
COMMENTS _____

FRIDAY, AUGUST 1   213

WHERE & WHEN _____ DISTANCE _____
COMMENTS _____

SATURDAY, AUGUST 2

WHERE & WHEN _____ DISTANCE _____
COMMENTS _____

SUNDAY, AUGUST 3

WHERE & WHEN _____ DISTANCE _____
COMMENTS _____

DISTANCE THIS WEEK _____WEIGHT _____

AUGUST

S	M	T	W	T	F	S
					1	2
3	4	5	6	7	8	9
10	11	12	13	14	15	16
17	18	19	20	21	22	23
24	25	26	27	28	29	30
31						

August: Like the Wind

The Chiricahua Apaches, who fought the final Indian wars on American soil in the last decades of the nineteenth century, were eventually rounded up and sent to concentration camps in Florida and Alabama. A quarter of their number died of disease in the first three years of their imprisonment; after five more debilitating years in the Deep South they were removed to Fort Sill, in Oklahoma.

When they got to Fort Sill they learned that mesquite trees, the beans of which had furnished a staple of their homeland diet and which they hadn't tasted in eight years, were growing forty-five miles away. They asked for and were given permission to harvest the beans. They left on foot and, walking and jogging the ninety-mile round-trip, returned forty-eight hours later, carrying three hundred bushels of the beans.

The Tarahumara Indians of Mexico, once implacable enemies of the Apaches, have well-deserved modern reputations as distance runners. They were known for running down deer and horses on foot, and may well have been superior to the Apaches in feats of endurance. But the Apaches were not exactly chopped liver. They preferred horseback, but war parties would sometimes go on foot to maintain the element of surprise, routinely covering forty to forty-five miles a day. When their horses had been stolen or killed by pursuing cavalry units, they would somehow maintain the same pace day after day, carrying their own supplies or living off the land—and taking their women and children with them. Geronimo once led a band of fugitives, including women and children and with virtually no food, for sixty nonstop miles, baffling their pursuers. During the period when they were still confined to reservations in Arizona, one of their white overseers was surprised when a sixty-year-old Apache woman approached him with a wild turkey in her arms, as a gift. She had run it down on foot.

These anecdotes come from *Once They Moved Like the Wind*, by David Roberts. In it, Roberts documents the training of Chiricahua youths, not only in the arts of hunting and warfare but specifically in physical fitness. "A boy's fitness training began in earnest at age eight," Roberts says. "He would be forced to get up before dawn to run to the top of a mountain and back before sunrise. He might run as far as four miles with a mouthful of water he was not allowed to swallow, or with his mouth full of pebbles. 'Your legs are your friends,' his mentors would tell the boy; after a meal he was supposed to rub grease on them to 'feed' his legs. . . . As a kind of graduation exam, a boy undertook a two-day cross-country run without food or sleep." A little more rigorous than my last preparation for a 10-K, I admit, but then I've never had the U.S. Cavalry chasing me. Geronimo did—five thousand of them in one campaign, plus three thousand Mexican soldiers and assorted scouts and volunteers, a force totaling, according to Roberts, "nearly nine thousand armed men pursuing eighteen Chiricahua warriors, thirteen women, and six children." They pursued the fugitives for five months, over something like three thousand miles, and captured not a single Apache.

Now that, folks, is distance running.

"Keep a diary and one day it'll keep you."

—MAE WEST

MONDAY, AUGUST 4 216

WHERE & WHEN _____ DISTANCE _____
COMMENTS _____

TUESDAY, AUGUST 5 217

WHERE & WHEN _____ DISTANCE _____
COMMENTS _____

WEDNESDAY, AUGUST 6 218

WHERE & WHEN _____ DISTANCE _____
COMMENTS _____

THURSDAY, AUGUST 7 219

WHERE & WHEN _____ DISTANCE _____
COMMENTS _____

FRIDAY, AUGUST 8 220

WHERE & WHEN _____ DISTANCE _____
COMMENTS _____

WHERE & WHEN _____ DISTANCE _____
COMMENTS _____

WHERE & WHEN _____ DISTANCE _____
COMMENTS _____

At night, face traffic and be prepared to bail out: ditches are softer
than cars.

"Mae West is a plumber's conception of Cleopatra."   —W. C. FIELDS

MONDAY, AUGUST 11   223

WHERE & WHEN _____ DISTANCE _____
COMMENTS _____

TUESDAY, AUGUST 12   224

WHERE & WHEN _____ DISTANCE _____
COMMENTS _____

WEDNESDAY, AUGUST 13   225

WHERE & WHEN _____ DISTANCE _____
COMMENTS _____

THURSDAY, AUGUST 14   226

WHERE & WHEN _____ DISTANCE _____
COMMENTS _____

FRIDAY, AUGUST 15   227

WHERE & WHEN _____ DISTANCE _____
COMMENTS _____

WHERE & WHEN ——————————————————— DISTANCE ————
COMMENTS ——————————————————————————————

SUNDAY, AUGUST 17

229

WHERE & WHEN ——————————————————— DISTANCE ————
COMMENTS ——————————————————————————————

The inflammation from damage to muscle tissue doesn't peak until
five days after injury.

DISTANCE THIS WEEK ———————————————— WEIGHT ————————

"My heart is pure as the driven slush."   —TALLULAH BANKHEAD

MONDAY, AUGUST 18   230

WHERE & WHEN _____ DISTANCE _____
COMMENTS _____

TUESDAY, AUGUST 19   231

WHERE & WHEN _____ DISTANCE _____
COMMENTS _____

WEDNESDAY, AUGUST 20   232

WHERE & WHEN _____ DISTANCE _____
COMMENTS _____

THURSDAY, AUGUST 21   233

WHERE & WHEN _____ DISTANCE _____
COMMENTS _____

FRIDAY, AUGUST 22   234

WHERE & WHEN _____ DISTANCE _____
COMMENTS _____

SATURDAY, AUGUST 23   235

WHERE & WHEN _____ DISTANCE _____
COMMENTS _____

SUNDAY, AUGUST 24   236

WHERE & WHEN _____ DISTANCE _____
COMMENTS _____

DISTANCE THIS WEEK _____ WEIGHT _____

"Man is a puny, slow, awkward, unarmed animal." —JACOB BRONOWSKI

MONDAY, AUGUST 25   237

WHERE & WHEN _____ DISTANCE _____
COMMENTS _____

TUESDAY, AUGUST 26   238

WHERE & WHEN _____ DISTANCE _____
COMMENTS _____

WEDNESDAY, AUGUST 27   239

WHERE & WHEN _____ DISTANCE _____
COMMENTS _____

THURSDAY, AUGUST 28   240

WHERE & WHEN _____ DISTANCE _____
COMMENTS _____

FRIDAY, AUGUST 29   241

WHERE & WHEN _____ DISTANCE _____
COMMENTS _____

SATURDAY, AUGUST 30   242

WHERE & WHEN _____ DISTANCE _____
COMMENTS _____

SUNDAY, AUGUST 31   243

WHERE & WHEN _____ DISTANCE _____
COMMENTS _____

Got a cold? If symptoms are above the neck and running doesn't
hurt, go ahead; if symptoms are below the neck, wait
until you're better.

DISTANCE THIS WEEK _____ WEIGHT _____

SEPTEMBER

S	M	T	W	T	F	S
	1 LABOR DAY	2	3	4	5	6
7	8	9	10	11	12	13
14	15	16	17	18	19	20
21	22	23	24	25	26	27
28	29	30				

September: Healing

It was my misfortune recently to be poked in the eye with a sharp stick. Literally: I was mowing, and a low branch somehow got behind my safety glasses. I was extremely lucky—no damage to vision, just a painful couple of hours and then a gradual return to normal over the next few days. Each day the swelling and redness would diminish, which was interesting to watch, and of course extremely reassuring. Healing, even of minor injuries, is always a thrilling small miracle.

I've long been fascinated with the connection between rehabilitation and athletic training, which are really two sides of the same coin. After surgery, or an injury of an orthopedic nature, the physical therapist usually devises an extremely specific piece of training, aimed at the exact site of the damage. Call it micro-managed training: the aim is to stimulate the damaged tissue to strengthen itself—or to re-strengthen itself, rather—to pre-trauma levels. (And if you choose to continue the rehab until the tissue is stronger than before the injury, nobody's going to complain, are they?) The stimulus of choice—because it's the only one that really works—is stress, which is another term for training.

This can be a tricky business. As my wife observed while I was still holding an ice pack to my eye, some people consider training to be a kind of controlled damage. The line between stress sufficient to stimulate strengthening and stress sufficient to reinjure can be a fine one. We are working, always, with Hans Selye's General Adaptation Syndrome, which posits a three-stage process: alarm, resistance, and exhaustion. The alarm stage is the injury itself; the resistance stage is training—all of athletic training, all of rehabilitation; the exhaustion stage is where reinjury occurs.

Tendon injuries provide the classic case. Tendons don't heal properly unless they are rehabilitated with regularly applied tension. Tendons are bundles of microscopic fibers, which rupture when the tendon is injured. As healing takes place, new fibers are laid down, but in a squiggly mess, like a plate of spaghetti rather than the cable-like structure they should be. (This is called scar tissue.)

Just the right amount of tension during the healing process realigns the fibers; too much tension re-ruptures them, reopening the original injury. Tendinitis sufferers often get into an endless cycle of rehab and reinjury, particularly because once you begin to feel better, you just naturally start applying more tension. Attention must particularly be paid to Selye's third stage, exhaustion, for which the only cure is rest. Rest is actually the most valuable training tool of all—as long as you do the training to go with it.

But I think it is far too cynical, or pessimistic, to think of training as controlled damage. Instead, we might very well think of it—of regular, consistent, programmatic athletic training, one favorite form of which is distance running—as healing after you've already healed. It is the healing of injuries you may not know you have: the injuries of modern, sedentary, high-pressure life.

More important, training is a kind of healing of injuries you haven't suffered yet. Look at it this way: running is healing ahead of time, before the fact.

"Life is one long process of getting tired."

—SAMUEL BUTLER

MONDAY, SEPTEMBER 1   244

WHERE & WHEN _____ DISTANCE _____

COMMENTS _____

TUESDAY, SEPTEMBER 2   245

WHERE & WHEN _____ DISTANCE _____

COMMENTS _____

WEDNESDAY, SEPTEMBER 3   246

WHERE & WHEN _____ DISTANCE _____

COMMENTS _____

THURSDAY, SEPTEMBER 4   247

WHERE & WHEN _____ DISTANCE _____

COMMENTS _____

FRIDAY, SEPTEMBER 5   248

WHERE & WHEN _____ DISTANCE _____

COMMENTS _____

WHERE & WHEN _____ DISTANCE _____
COMMENTS _____

WHERE & WHEN _____ DISTANCE _____
COMMENTS _____

If you've suffered a thermal injury (heat stroke, heat exhaustion, hypothermia) in the past, you may be predisposed to similar injury in the future.

DISTANCE THIS WEEK _____ WEIGHT _____

"Principles have no real force except when one is well fed."

—MARK TWAIN

MONDAY, SEPTEMBER 8   251

WHERE & WHEN _____ DISTANCE _____

COMMENTS _____

TUESDAY, SEPTEMBER 9   252

WHERE & WHEN _____ DISTANCE _____

COMMENTS _____

WEDNESDAY, SEPTEMBER 10   253

WHERE & WHEN _____ DISTANCE _____

COMMENTS _____

THURSDAY, SEPTEMBER 11   254

WHERE & WHEN _____ DISTANCE _____

COMMENTS _____

FRIDAY, SEPTEMBER 12   255

WHERE & WHEN _____ DISTANCE _____

COMMENTS _____

WHERE & WHEN ⎯⎯⎯⎯⎯⎯⎯⎯⎯⎯ DISTANCE ⎯⎯⎯⎯⎯
COMMENTS ⎯⎯⎯⎯⎯⎯⎯⎯⎯⎯⎯⎯⎯⎯⎯⎯⎯⎯

WHERE & WHEN ⎯⎯⎯⎯⎯⎯⎯⎯⎯⎯ DISTANCE ⎯⎯⎯⎯⎯
COMMENTS ⎯⎯⎯⎯⎯⎯⎯⎯⎯⎯⎯⎯⎯⎯⎯⎯⎯⎯

Trim your toenails short and square; you'll run better for it.

"England has forty-two religions and only two sauces." —VOLTAIRE

MONDAY, SEPTEMBER 15   258

WHERE & WHEN _____ DISTANCE _____
COMMENTS _____

TUESDAY, SEPTEMBER 16   259

WHERE & WHEN _____ DISTANCE _____
COMMENTS _____

WEDNESDAY, SEPTEMBER 17   260

WHERE & WHEN _____ DISTANCE _____
COMMENTS _____

THURSDAY, SEPTEMBER 18   261

WHERE & WHEN _____ DISTANCE _____
COMMENTS _____

FRIDAY, SEPTEMBER 19   262

WHERE & WHEN _____ DISTANCE _____
COMMENTS _____

WHERE & WHEN _____ DISTANCE _____
COMMENTS _____

WHERE & WHEN _____ DISTANCE _____
COMMENTS _____

Run up the hill for your heart, down the hill for your legs.

DISTANCE THIS WEEK _____ WEIGHT _____

"I save energy by asking my servants not to turn on the self-cleaning oven after seven in the morning."
—BETSY BLOOMINGDALE

MONDAY, SEPTEMBER 22   265

WHERE & WHEN _____ DISTANCE _____
COMMENTS _____

TUESDAY, SEPTEMBER 23   266

WHERE & WHEN _____ DISTANCE _____
COMMENTS _____

WEDNESDAY, SEPTEMBER 24   267

WHERE & WHEN _____ DISTANCE _____
COMMENTS _____

THURSDAY, SEPTEMBER 25   268

WHERE & WHEN _____ DISTANCE _____
COMMENTS _____

FRIDAY, SEPTEMBER 26   269

WHERE & WHEN _____ DISTANCE _____
COMMENTS _____

WHERE & WHEN _____ DISTANCE _____

COMMENTS _____

WHERE & WHEN _____ DISTANCE _____

COMMENTS _____

Type A personalities injure themselves more than Type Bs.

OCTOBER

S	M	T	W	T	F	S
			1	2 ROSH HASHANAH	3	4
5	6	7	8	9	10	11 YOM KIPPUR
12 COLUMBUS DAY	13 COLUMBUS DAY OBSERVED	14	15	16	17	18
19	20	21	22	23	24 UNITED NATIONS DAY	25
26	27	28	29	30	31 HALLOWEEN	

October: Nine Habits of Highly Effective Rowers

Concept II, a maker of very fine rowing machines, publishes an excellent small magazine called *Ergo Update*. In it they have been publishing results from exercise physiologist Stephen Seiler's ongoing study of rowers between the ages of forty and eighty-five. Rowing isn't running, of course—rowing demands more strength, and heart rates are sometimes lower for the same individual rowing versus running at a given intensity—but the guidelines for an effective program in either activity are based on the same physiological principles. From the routines reported by their subjects, the researchers have gleaned a list of good habits for rowers, which could certainly apply as well to any other form of regular exercise. I found them quite interesting:

Begin with a goal in mind. What do you want to accomplish this week?, this month?, this year? Having a clear destination makes for a straighter path.

Find a training partner(s). At least once or twice a week, find someone to push you and be pushed by you. A running coach says, "Run alone and you learn to run hard and slow. Run with others, and you'll learn to be efficient and fast."

Use a heart rate monitor (at least on some days). This is your physiological tachometer. Use it to tune in to the relationship between effort and outcome.

Hit the weights. As we age we lose muscle mass; strength training can help prevent this. It is never too late to get stronger.

Record your workouts. When you improve, you will have a record of your personal "formula" for success.

Variety is a key to continued improvement. Bodies and minds grow stale very quickly from the same 30-minute workout every day.

Listen to your body. Stress is cumulative. Job, home, work, exercise, all can contribute. Let the occasional bad day remind you of how good the good days are.

Cycle your training. . . . Attempt to make weekly changes in either intensity, duration, or frequency, of 5 to 10 percent at most. The easier weeks are built in to help the body recover fully, and continue to improve.

Test yourself. . . . Every couple of weeks, challenge yourself to try something you have never done before, and record the results.

Sound advice. For further information, contact Steve Seiler or Waneen Spirduso, Masters Aging & Rowing Study, c/o Dept. of Kinesiology, University of Texas, Austin, TX 78712.

"Patience, n. *A minor form of despair, disguised as a virtue."*

—AMBROSE BIERCE

MONDAY, SEPTEMBER 29   272

WHERE & WHEN _____ DISTANCE _____
COMMENTS _____

TUESDAY, SEPTEMBER 30   273

WHERE & WHEN _____ DISTANCE _____
COMMENTS _____

WEDNESDAY, OCTOBER 1   274

WHERE & WHEN _____ DISTANCE _____
COMMENTS _____

THURSDAY, OCTOBER 2   275

WHERE & WHEN _____ DISTANCE _____
COMMENTS _____

FRIDAY, OCTOBER 3   276

WHERE & WHEN _____ DISTANCE _____
COMMENTS _____

WHERE & WHEN _____ DISTANCE _____

COMMENTS _____

WHERE & WHEN _____ DISTANCE _____

COMMENTS _____

Podiatrists say that if you're fated for overuse injuries, they're
likely to start at around thirty miles per week.

DISTANCE CARRIED FORWARD _____

"Liberty doesn't work as well in practice as it does in speeches."

—WILL ROGERS

MONDAY, OCTOBER 6   279

WHERE & WHEN _____ DISTANCE _____
COMMENTS _____

TUESDAY, OCTOBER 7   280

WHERE & WHEN _____ DISTANCE _____
COMMENTS _____

WEDNESDAY, OCTOBER 8   281

WHERE & WHEN _____ DISTANCE _____
COMMENTS _____

THURSDAY, OCTOBER 9   282

WHERE & WHEN _____ DISTANCE _____
COMMENTS _____

FRIDAY, OCTOBER 10   283

WHERE & WHEN _____ DISTANCE _____
COMMENTS _____

SATURDAY, OCTOBER 11

WHERE & WHEN _____ DISTANCE _____

COMMENTS _____

SUNDAY, OCTOBER 12

WHERE & WHEN _____ DISTANCE _____

COMMENTS _____

Checking your weight and pulse rate upon arising is a good idea: a
rise in resting pulse rate means you ought to ease up, particularly
if you're pushing hard or are under stress.

DISTANCE THIS WEEK _____ WEIGHT _____

"As American as English muffins and French toast."

—JOHN RUSSELL TAYLOR

MONDAY, OCTOBER 13 286

WHERE & WHEN _____ DISTANCE _____

COMMENTS _____

TUESDAY, OCTOBER 14 287

WHERE & WHEN _____ DISTANCE _____

COMMENTS _____

WEDNESDAY, OCTOBER 15 288

WHERE & WHEN _____ DISTANCE _____

COMMENTS _____

THURSDAY, OCTOBER 16 289

WHERE & WHEN _____ DISTANCE _____

COMMENTS _____

FRIDAY, OCTOBER 17 290

WHERE & WHEN _____ DISTANCE _____

COMMENTS _____

WHERE & WHEN _____ DISTANCE _____
COMMENTS _____

WHERE & WHEN _____ DISTANCE _____
COMMENTS _____

For every pound of glycogen you store away—as from carbo-
loading—you gain three pounds of water.

"One might say that the American trend of education is to reduce the sense almost to nil."
—ISADORA DUNCAN

MONDAY, OCTOBER 20 293

WHERE & WHEN _____ DISTANCE _____
COMMENTS _____

TUESDAY, OCTOBER 21 294

WHERE & WHEN _____ DISTANCE _____
COMMENTS _____

WEDNESDAY, OCTOBER 22 295

WHERE & WHEN _____ DISTANCE _____
COMMENTS _____

THURSDAY, OCTOBER 23 296

WHERE & WHEN _____ DISTANCE _____
COMMENTS _____

FRIDAY, OCTOBER 24 297

WHERE & WHEN _____ DISTANCE _____
COMMENTS _____

WHERE & WHEN _____ DISTANCE _____
COMMENTS _____

SUNDAY, OCTOBER 26   299

WHERE & WHEN _____ DISTANCE _____
COMMENTS _____

Trouble relaxing as you run? Start with the face muscles—or the
forehead—and work downward.

"What contemptible scoundrel stole the cork from my lunch?"

—W. C. FIELDS

MONDAY, OCTOBER 27   300

WHERE & WHEN _____ DISTANCE _____
COMMENTS _____

TUESDAY, OCTOBER 28   301

WHERE & WHEN _____ DISTANCE _____
COMMENTS _____

WEDNESDAY, OCTOBER 29   302

WHERE & WHEN _____ DISTANCE _____
COMMENTS _____

THURSDAY, OCTOBER 30   303

WHERE & WHEN _____ DISTANCE _____
COMMENTS _____

FRIDAY, OCTOBER 31   304

WHERE & WHEN _____ DISTANCE _____
COMMENTS _____

SATURDAY, NOVEMBER 1

305

WHERE & WHEN ———————————————— DISTANCE ————
COMMENTS ———————————————————————————

SUNDAY, NOVEMBER 2

306

WHERE & WHEN ———————————————— DISTANCE ————
COMMENTS ———————————————————————————

DISTANCE THIS WEEK ————————————— WEIGHT ————————

NOVEMBER

S	M	T	W	T	F	S
						1
2	3	4 ELECTION DAY	5	6	7	8
9	10	11 VETERANS DAY	12	13	14	15
16	17	18	19	20	21	22
23	24	25	26	27 THANKSGIVING DAY	28	29
30						

November: Fit Biz

The greatest unsolved problem in the world of physical fitness—after, perhaps, the depressingly predictable return of all that weight you so painfully lost—is how to get people to continue with their exercise programs. "Compliance," the phys ed types like to call it. It's easy enough to get them started—particularly, for some reason, in September and February—but keeping them going is a terrible problem. The dirty little secret of the so-called fitness revolution is that eight out of ten exercisers drop out within ninety days of starting.

Call the high drop-out rate the lemon in the exercise equation; predictably enough—just like the return of those love handles—it has created a lemonade industry. A cynic who is in the business explained to me how it works. You start up a fitness club, selling memberships at a stiff price—lifetime memberships, if possible—and then depend on the drop-out rate to relieve you of the expensive task of providing service to the members. If members defy statistics and persist in using your club, you discourage them by shutting down the convenient facility they joined, for example, and "transferring" their memberships to another facility on the other side of town. This tends to bring the statistics back into line.

It's not clear how many fitness clubs there are—or how many of them are sincerely in the business of helping you shape up—but counting everything from the local Y through health spas and figure salons on up to the hyper-exclusive, hyper-expensive fat farms for the ultra-privileged, there are at least fifteen hundred different organizations in this country selling fitness. (This does not include the publishing industry, which sometimes seems to be surviving on diet books and exercise manuals.) Nobody had dreamed there were that many such organizations until the federal government began investigating them. The fitness industry formed a lobbying group for self-protection, and that's how many joined up.

The feds started looking into the fitness organizations because so many of them seemed to be set up to harvest the ninety-day drop-out principle. Somehow the feds suspected this was a scam. In fact, it is such a good one that the fraternity of scam artists who have made it into really big money in recent years has become populated by a high percentage of muscular, well-tanned, ultra-trim swindlers whose sunny good looks are part and parcel of the promotional kit.

The health club scam has recently been overshadowed by a subtler form of bunco, the exercise machine. For about the price of a one-year membership you can have a gadget in your own home that relieves you of the tedious process of getting into your car and driving down to the club to use someone else's. I know households that have bought, serially, four or five of the things. Some of the machines even see occasional use.

This sardonic view of how the industry really works certainly gave me a lot of food for thought. Detroit never really took off as a marketing miracle until it invented planned—"dynamic"—obsolescence. Here you have the same idea turned upside down: a constant turnover, 80 percent all new people every ninety days. A renewable market. *Customer* obsolescence. Wonderful.

"Conscience and cowardice are really the same things. Conscience is the trade name of the firm." —OSCAR WILDE

MONDAY, NOVEMBER 3 307

WHERE & WHEN _____ DISTANCE _____
COMMENTS _____

TUESDAY, NOVEMBER 4 308

WHERE & WHEN _____ DISTANCE _____
COMMENTS _____

WEDNESDAY, NOVEMBER 5 309

WHERE & WHEN _____ DISTANCE _____
COMMENTS _____

THURSDAY, NOVEMBER 6 310

WHERE & WHEN _____ DISTANCE _____
COMMENTS _____

FRIDAY, NOVEMBER 7 311

WHERE & WHEN _____ DISTANCE _____
COMMENTS _____

SATURDAY, NOVEMBER 8   312

WHERE & WHEN _____ DISTANCE _____
COMMENTS _____

SUNDAY, NOVEMBER 9   313

WHERE & WHEN _____ DISTANCE _____
COMMENTS _____

Alcohol dilates the blood vessels, speeding heat loss.

DISTANCE THIS WEEK _____ WEIGHT _____

"There is no reason for any individual to have a computer in their home."
—KEN OLSON, 1977

MONDAY, NOVEMBER 10   314

WHERE & WHEN _____ DISTANCE _____
COMMENTS _____

TUESDAY, NOVEMBER 11   315

WHERE & WHEN _____ DISTANCE _____
COMMENTS _____

WEDNESDAY, NOVEMBER 12   316

WHERE & WHEN _____ DISTANCE _____
COMMENTS _____

THURSDAY, NOVEMBER 13   317

WHERE & WHEN _____ DISTANCE _____
COMMENTS _____

FRIDAY, NOVEMBER 14   318

WHERE & WHEN _____ DISTANCE _____
COMMENTS _____

WHERE & WHEN _____ DISTANCE _____
COMMENTS _____

WHERE & WHEN _____ DISTANCE _____
COMMENTS _____

A five-day layoff won't hurt your physical conditioning, but the
mental part can be another matter.

DISTANCE THIS WEEK _____ WEIGHT _____

"The balls used in top-class games are generally smaller than those used in others."
—PAUL FUSSELL

MONDAY, NOVEMBER 17   321

WHERE & WHEN _____ DISTANCE _____
COMMENTS _____

TUESDAY, NOVEMBER 18   322

WHERE & WHEN _____ DISTANCE _____
COMMENTS _____

WEDNESDAY, NOVEMBER 19   323

WHERE & WHEN _____ DISTANCE _____
COMMENTS _____

THURSDAY, NOVEMBER 20   324

WHERE & WHEN _____ DISTANCE _____
COMMENTS _____

FRIDAY, NOVEMBER 21   325

WHERE & WHEN _____ DISTANCE _____
COMMENTS _____

SATURDAY, NOVEMBER 22

WHERE & WHEN _____ DISTANCE _____

COMMENTS _____

SUNDAY, NOVEMBER 23

WHERE & WHEN _____ DISTANCE _____

COMMENTS _____

Exercise is cumulative: several short sessions do as much as
one long one.

DISTANCE THIS WEEK _____ WEIGHT _____

"As elaborate a waste of human intelligence as you can find outside an advertising agency."
—RAYMOND CHANDLER

MONDAY, NOVEMBER 24   328

WHERE & WHEN _____ DISTANCE _____
COMMENTS _____

TUESDAY, NOVEMBER 25   329

WHERE & WHEN _____ DISTANCE _____
COMMENTS _____

WEDNESDAY, NOVEMBER 26   330

WHERE & WHEN _____ DISTANCE _____
COMMENTS _____

THURSDAY, NOVEMBER 27   331

WHERE & WHEN _____ DISTANCE _____
COMMENTS _____

FRIDAY, NOVEMBER 28   332

WHERE & WHEN _____ DISTANCE _____
COMMENTS _____

SATURDAY, NOVEMBER 29   333

WHERE & WHEN _____ DISTANCE _____

COMMENTS _____

SUNDAY, NOVEMBER 30   334

WHERE & WHEN _____ DISTANCE _____

COMMENTS _____

In summer, a light-colored hat can help a lot.

DISTANCE THIS WEEK _____ WEIGHT _____

DECEMBER

S	M	T	W	T	F	S
	1	2	3	4	5	6
7	8	9	10	11	12	13
14	15	16	17	18	19	20
21	22	23	24 HANUKKAH	25 CHRISTMAS DAY	26 BOXING DAY (CANADA)	27
28	29	30	31			

December: Gwen's Oatmeal Cookies

For those of us who run to eat, December is sugarplum time (although I should here confess that I've never actually seen or tasted a sugarplum). No matter how carefully we've obeyed this year's strictures of the food police, it is carbo-loading month. Go ahead, fill up, what the heck. We'll run it off in January.

Should anyone's appetite begin to flag, I recommend Patrick O'Brian's Aubrey/Maturin series of historical novels about the nineteenth-century British navy. Woven among the daring sea adventures and international intrigues is a carefully researched picture of shipboard life, up to and including the bill of fare. Long stretches of that life may be nutritionally marginal—scurvy is seldom more than a few weeks off—but when proper food is available it is taken advantage of, and O'Brian never fails to supply the menu, not to mention the wine lists. The desserts alone, for some reason in those days all called "puddings" by the English, make an appetite-whetting list, although some of the nineteenth-century names—Dead Baby, Spotted Dick—may put you off a little. Personally, I even relish the toasted cheese (usually served with port) with which our heroes top off their evening shipboard chamber-music duets: Captain Jack Aubrey on violin and ship's surgeon (and master spy) Stephen Maturin on cello.

I am not by any stretch of the imagination a cook, but I did inherit one recipe that I try to prepare each holiday season. My mother's oatmeal cookies were a staple in the household—a somewhat stingy household except where desserts were concerned—and my own children grew up on them. Those children, now adult and scattered across the country, may well dread the packages of cookies that will arrive in the next couple of weeks, but they're too polite to say so. I don't care: I love them (the cookies, as well as the offspring), and am now attempting to promote a fondness for same in all the grandchildren here and to come. As cookies they have the cardinal virtue of not being terribly sweet. That means you can eat a lot of them at one sitting, which—see carbo-loading, above—is what December is all about.

1 cup raisins, plumped	*2 cups flour*
1 cup shortening	*2 cups quick oats*
1 cup sugar	*1 teaspoon cinnamon*
3 eggs, beaten	*$\frac{1}{2}$ teaspoon salt*
$\frac{1}{2}$ cup chopped nuts	*$\frac{1}{2}$ teaspoon allspice*
$\frac{1}{2}$ teaspoon baking soda	*$\frac{1}{2}$ teaspoon cloves*
6 tablespoons water in which the raisins have simmered	

Simmer raisins under cover for five minutes, drain, put aside, saving 6 tablespoons of liquid. Cream shortening, sugar; add eggs and mix well. Add mixed dry ingredients alternately with liquid, then nuts and raisins. Drop by spoonfuls on greased cookie sheet and bake at 400° for 10–12 minutes. Makes 3–4 dozen cookies. Personally, I recommend three or four of them, with a glass of cold milk, after every December run. Happy holidays.

"Bore, n. A person who talks when you wish him to listen."
—AMBROSE BIERCE

MONDAY, DECEMBER 1   335

WHERE & WHEN _____ DISTANCE _____
COMMENTS _____

TUESDAY, DECEMBER 2   336

WHERE & WHEN _____ DISTANCE _____
COMMENTS _____

WEDNESDAY, DECEMBER 3   337

WHERE & WHEN _____ DISTANCE _____
COMMENTS _____

THURSDAY, DECEMBER 4   338

WHERE & WHEN _____ DISTANCE _____
COMMENTS _____

FRIDAY, DECEMBER 5   339

WHERE & WHEN _____ DISTANCE _____
COMMENTS _____

SATURDAY, DECEMBER 6

340

WHERE & WHEN _____ DISTANCE _____

COMMENTS _____

SUNDAY, DECEMBER 7

341

WHERE & WHEN _____ DISTANCE _____

COMMENTS _____

That ringing in your ears from too much aspirin can actually lead
to hearing loss.

DISTANCE THIS WEEK _____ WEIGHT _____

"The doctor has been taught to be interested not in health but in disease. What the public is taught is that health is the cure for disease."
—ASHLEY MONTAGU

MONDAY, DECEMBER 8 — 342

WHERE & WHEN _____ DISTANCE _____
COMMENTS _____

TUESDAY, DECEMBER 9 — 343

WHERE & WHEN _____ DISTANCE _____
COMMENTS _____

WEDNESDAY, DECEMBER 10 — 344

WHERE & WHEN _____ DISTANCE _____
COMMENTS _____

THURSDAY, DECEMBER 11 — 345

WHERE & WHEN _____ DISTANCE _____
COMMENTS _____

FRIDAY, DECEMBER 12 — 346

WHERE & WHEN _____ DISTANCE _____
COMMENTS _____

WHERE & WHEN _____ DISTANCE _____
COMMENTS _____

WHERE & WHEN _____ DISTANCE _____
COMMENTS _____

If you must sauna, cool down completely first. Inflammation is
heat; that's why trainers put ice on injuries.

"Convictions are more dangerous enemies of truth than lies."

—NIETZSCHE

MONDAY, DECEMBER 15   349

WHERE & WHEN _____ DISTANCE _____
COMMENTS _____

TUESDAY, DECEMBER 16   350

WHERE & WHEN _____ DISTANCE _____
COMMENTS _____

WEDNESDAY, DECEMBER 17   351

WHERE & WHEN _____ DISTANCE _____
COMMENTS _____

THURSDAY, DECEMBER 18   352

WHERE & WHEN _____ DISTANCE _____
COMMENTS _____

FRIDAY, DECEMBER 19   353

WHERE & WHEN _____ DISTANCE _____
COMMENTS _____

WHERE & WHEN _____ DISTANCE _____

COMMENTS _____

WHERE & WHEN _____ DISTANCE _____

COMMENTS _____

"One of the most common of all diseases is diagnosis." —JULIAN HUXLEY

MONDAY, DECEMBER 22   356

WHERE & WHEN _____ DISTANCE _____
COMMENTS _____

TUESDAY, DECEMBER 23   357

WHERE & WHEN _____ DISTANCE _____
COMMENTS _____

WEDNESDAY, DECEMBER 24   358

WHERE & WHEN _____ DISTANCE _____
COMMENTS _____

THURSDAY, DECEMBER 25   359

WHERE & WHEN _____ DISTANCE _____
COMMENTS _____

FRIDAY, DECEMBER 26   360

WHERE & WHEN _____ DISTANCE _____
COMMENTS _____

WHERE & WHEN _____ DISTANCE _____

COMMENTS _____

WHERE & WHEN _____ DISTANCE _____

COMMENTS _____

If you start shivering when you slow down, immediately seek
shelter and warmth: you're approaching hypothermia.

"The meaning of life is that it stops."

—FRANZ KAFKA

MONDAY, DECEMBER 29 363

WHERE & WHEN _____ DISTANCE _____
COMMENTS_____

TUESDAY, DECEMBER 30 364

WHERE & WHEN _____ DISTANCE _____
COMMENTS_____

WEDNESDAY, DECEMBER 31 365

WHERE & WHEN _____ DISTANCE _____
COMMENTS_____

THURSDAY, JANUARY 1 1

WHERE & WHEN _____ DISTANCE _____
COMMENTS_____

FRIDAY, JANUARY 2 2

WHERE & WHEN _____ DISTANCE _____
COMMENTS_____

WHERE & WHEN ————————————————— DISTANCE ————
COMMENTS ————————————————————————————

WHERE & WHEN ————————————————— DISTANCE ————
COMMENTS ————————————————————————————

Injuries of any kind heal faster with sleep.

DISTANCE THIS WEEK ————————————————— WEIGHT ————————

Twelve Months of Running

JAN. 6	JAN. 13	JAN. 20	JAN. 27	FEB. 3	FEB. 10	FEB. 17	FEB. 24	MARCH 3	MARCH 10	MARCH 17	MARCH 24	MARCH 31

To create a cumulative bar graph of weekly mileage, apply an appropriate scale at the left-hand margin. Then fill in the bar for each week of running.

APR. 7	APR. 14	APR. 21	APR. 28	MAY 5	MAY 12	MAY 19	MAY 26	JUNE 2	JUNE 9	JUNE 16	JUNE 23	JUNE 30

To create a cumulative bar graph of weekly mileage, apply an appropriate scale at the left-hand margin. Then fill in the bar for each week of running.

JULY 7	JULY 14	JULY 21	JULY 28	AUG. 4	AUG. 11	AUG. 18	AUG. 25	SEPT. 1	SEPT. 8	SEPT. 15	SEPT. 22	SEPT. 29

To create a cumulative bar graph of weekly mileage, apply an appropriate scale at the left-hand margin. Then fill in the bar for each week of running.

OCT. 6	OCT. 13	OCT. 20	OCT. 27	NOV. 3	NOV. 10	NOV. 17	NOV. 24	DEC. 1	DEC. 8	DEC. 15	DEC. 22	DEC. 29

A Record of Races

DATE	PLACE	DISTANCE	TIME	PACE	COMMENTS AND EXCUSES

A Record of Races

DATE	PLACE	DISTANCE	TIME	PACE	COMMENTS AND EXCUSES

Marathon Quick Reference Split Times*

Mile	1	2	3	4	5	6	7	8	
PACE									PACE
2:04	4:44	9:28	14:11	18:55	23:39	28:23	33:07	37:50	2:04
2:05	4:46	9:32	14:18	19:08	23:51	28:37	33:23	38:09	2:05
2:06	4:48	9:36	14:26	19:14	24:03	28:51	33:40	38:29	2:06
2:07	4:51	9:42	14:33	19:24	24:15	29:06	33:57	38:48	2:07
2:08	4:53	9:48	14:40	19:34	24:27	29:20	34:14	39:07	2:08
2:09	4:55	9:50	14:46	19:41	24:36	29:31	34:26	39:21	2:09
2:10	4:58	9:55	14:53	19:50	24:48	29:46	34:43	39:41	2:10
2:11	5:00	10:00	15:00	20:00	25:00	30:00	35:00	40:00	2:11
2:12	5:02	10:04	15:06	20:12	25:14	30:16	35:18	40:20	2:12
2:13	5:05	10:10	15:14	20:19	25:24	30:29	35:34	40:38	2:13
2:14	5:07	10:13	15:20	20:26	25:33	30:40	35:46	40:53	2:14
2:15	5:09	10:18	15:27	20:36	25:45	30:54	36:03	41:12	2:15
2:16	5:11	10:23	15:34	20:46	25:57	31:08	36:20	41:31	2:16
2:17	5:14	10:28	15:41	20:55	26:09	31:23	36:37	41:50	2:17
2:18	5:16	10:32	15:49	21:05	26:21	31:37	36:53	42:10	2:18
2:19	5:18	10:36	15:54	21:12	26:30	31:48	37:06	42:24	2:19
2:20	5:21	10:41	16:01	21:22	26:42	32:02	37:23	42:43	2:20
2:21	5:23	10:46	16:09	21:31	26:54	32:17	37:40	43:02	2:21
2:22	5:25	10:50	16:16	21:41	27:06	32:31	37:56	43:22	2:22
2:23	5:28	10:55	16:23	21:50	27:18	32:46	38:13	43:41	2:23
2:24	5:30	11:00	16:30	22:00	27:30	33:00	38:30	44:00	2:24
2:25	5:32	11:04	16:35	22:07	27:39	33:11	38:43	44:14	2:25
2:26	5:34	11:08	16:42	22:17	27:51	33:25	38:59	44:34	2:26
2:27	5:37	11:13	16:50	22:26	28:03	33:40	39:16	44:53	2:27
2:28	5:39	11:18	16:57	22:36	28:15	33:54	39:33	45:12	2:28
2:29	5:41	11:23	17:04	22:46	28:27	34:08	39:50	45:31	2:29
2:30	5:44	11:28	17:11	22:55	28:39	34:23	40:07	45:50	2:30
2:35	5:55	11:50	17:46	23:41	29:36	35:31	41:26	47:22	2:35
2:40	6:07	12:13	18:20	24:26	30:33	36:40	42:46	48:53	2:40
2:45	6:18	12:36	18:54	25:12	31:30	37:48	44:06	50:24	2:45
2:50	6:29	12:59	19:28	25:58	32:27	38:56	45:26	51:55	2:50
2:55	6:41	13:22	20:02	26:43	33:24	40:05	46:46	53:26	2:55
3:00	6:52	13:44	20:37	27:29	34:21	41:23	48:05	54:58	3:00
3:15	7:26	14:53	22:19	29:46	37:12	44:38	52:05	59:52	3:15
3:30	8:01	16:02	24:04	32:05	40:06	48:07	56:08	1:04:10	3:30
3:45	8:35	17:11	25:46	34:22	42:57	51:32	1:00:08	1:08:43	3:45
4:00	9:10	18:19	27:29	36:38	45:48	54:57	1:04:07	1:13:17	4:00
4:15	9:44	19:28	29:11	38:55	48:39	58:23	1:08:07	1:17:50	4:15
4:30	10:18	20:36	30:54	41:12	51:30	1:01:48	1:12:06	1:22:24	4:30
4:45	10:53	21:46	32:38	43:31	54:24	1:05:17	1:16:10	1:27:02	4:45
5:00	11:27	22:54	34:21	45:48	57:15	1:08:42	1:20:09	1:31:36	5:00

*Times are rounded off to accommodate fractions of a second.

Mile	9	10	11	12	13	14	15	
PACE								PACE
2:04	42:34	47:18	52:02	56:46	1:01:29	1:06:13	1:10:57	2:04
2:05	42:56	47:42	52:28	57:14	1:02:06	1:06:52	1:11:36	2:05
2:06	43:17	48:06	52:55	57:43	1:02:32	1:07:20	1:12:09	2:06
2:07	43:39	48:30	53:21	58:12	1:03:03	1:07:54	1:12:45	2:07
2:08	44:00	48:54	53:47	58:41	1:03:11	1:08:27	1:13:30	2:08
2:09	44:17	49:12	54:07	59:02	1:03:58	1:08:53	1:13:48	2:09
2:10	44:38	49:36	54:34	59:31	1:04:29	1:09:26	1:14:24	2:10
2:11	45:00	50:00	55:00	1:00:00	1:05:00	1:10:00	1:15:00	2:11
2:12	45:22	50:24	55:26	1:00:28	1:05:30	1:10:32	1:15:34	2:12
2:13	45:43	50:48	55:53	1:00:58	1:06:02	1:11:07	1:16:12	2:13
2:14	46:00	51:06	56:13	1:01:19	1:06:26	1:11:32	1:16:39	2:14
2:15	46:21	51:30	56:39	1:01:48	1:06:57	1:12:06	1:17:15	2:15
2:16	46:43	51:54	57:05	1:02:17	1:07:28	1:12:40	1:17:51	2:16
2:17	47:04	52:18	57:32	1:02:46	1:08:00	1:13:13	1:18:27	2:17
2:18	47:26	52:42	57:58	1:03:14	1:08:31	1:13:47	1:19:03	2:18
2:19	47:42	53:00	58:18	1:03:36	1:08:54	1:14:12	1:19:30	2:19
2:20	48:04	53:24	58:44	1:04:05	1:09:25	1:14:46	1:20:06	2:20
2:21	48:25	53:48	59:11	1:04:34	1:09:56	1:15:19	1:20:42	2:21
2:22	48:47	54:12	59:37	1:05:02	1:10:28	1:15:53	1:21:18	2:22
2:23	49:08	54:36	1:00:04	1:05:31	1:10:59	1:16:26	1:21:54	2:23
2:24	49:30	55:00	1:00:30	1:06:00	1:11:30	1:17:00	1:22:30	2:24
2:25	49:46	55:18	1:00:50	1:06:22	1:11:53	1:17:25	1:22:57	2:25
2:26	50:08	55:42	1:01:16	1:06:50	1:12:25	1:17:59	1:23:33	2:26
2:27	50:29	56:06	1:01:42	1:07:19	1:12:56	1:18:32	1:24:09	2:27
2:28	50:51	56:30	1:02:09	1:07:48	1:13:27	1:19:06	1:24:45	2:28
2:29	51:13	56:54	1:02:35	1:08:17	1:13:58	1:19:40	1:25:21	2:29
2:30	51:34	57:18	1:03:02	1:08:46	1:14:47	1:20:13	1:25:57	2:30
2:35	53:17	59:12	1:05:07	1:11:02	1:16:58	1:22:53	1:28:48	2:35
2:40	54:59	1:01:06	1:07:13	1:13:19	1:19:26	1:25:32	1:31:39	2:40
2:45	56:42	1:03:00	1:09:18	1:15:36	1:21:54	1:28:12	1:34:30	2:45
2:50	58:25	1:04:54	1:11:23	1:17:53	1:24:22	1:30:52	1:37:21	2:50
2:55	1:00:07	1:06:48	1:13:29	1:20:10	1:26:50	1:33:31	1:40:12	2:55
3:00	1:01:50	1:08:42	1:15:34	1:22:26	1:29:19	1:36:11	1:43:03	3:00
3:15	1:06:58	1:14:24	1:21:50	1:29:17	1:36:43	1:44:10	1:51:36	3:15
3:30	1:12:11	1:20:12	1:28:13	1:36:14	1:44:16	1:52:17	2:00:18	3:30
3:45	1:17:19	1:25:54	1:34:29	1:43:05	1:51:40	2:00:16	2:08:51	3:45
4:00	1:22:26	1:31:36	1:40:46	1:49:55	1:59:05	2:08:14	2:17:24	4:00
4:15	1:27:34	1:37:18	1:47:02	1:56:46	2:06:29	2:16:13	2:25:57	4:15
4:30	1:32:42	1:43:00	1:53:18	2:03:36	2:13:54	2:24:12	2:34:30	4:30
4:45	1:37:55	1:48:48	1:59:41	2:10:34	2:21:26	2:32:19	2:43:12	4:45
5:00	1:43:03	1:54:30	2:05:57	2:17:24	2:28:51	2:40:18	2:51:45	5:00

*Times are rounded off to accommodate fractions of a second.

Mile	16	17	18	19	20	21	22	
PACE								PACE
2:04	1:15:41	1:20:25	1:25:08	1:29:52	1:34:36	1:39:20	1:44:04	2:04
2:05	1:16:19	1:21:05	1:25:51	1:30:37	1:35:24	1:40:10	1:44:56	2:05
2:06	1:16:58	1:21:46	1:26:35	1:31:23	1:36:12	1:41:06	1:45:49	2:06
2:07	1:17:36	1:22:27	1:27:18	1:32:09	1:37:00	1:41:51	1:46:42	2:07
2:08	1:18:14	1:23:08	1:28:12	1:32:55	1:37:48	1:42:41	1:47:35	2:08
2:09	1:18:43	1:23:38	1:28:34	1:33:29	1:38:24	1:43:19	1:48:14	2:09
2:10	1:19:22	1:24:19	1:29:17	1:34:14	1:39:12	1:44:10	1:49:07	2:10
2:11	1:20:00	1:25:00	1:30:00	1:35:00	1:40:00	1:45:00	1:50:00	2:11
2:12	1:20:36	1:25:38	1:30:40	1:35:42	1:40:46	1:45:48	1:50:50	2:12
2:13	1:21:17	1:26:22	1:31:26	1:36:31	1:41:36	1:46:41	1:51:46	2:13
2:14	1:21:46	1:26:52	1:31:58	1:37:05	1:42:12	1:47:19	1:52:25	2:14
2:15	1:22:24	1:27:33	1:32:42	1:37:51	1:43:00	1:48:09	1:53:18	2:15
2:16	1:23:02	1:28:14	1:33:25	1:38:37	1:43:48	1:48:59	1:54:11	2:16
2:17	1:23:41	1:28:55	1:34:08	1:39:22	1:44:36	1:49:50	1:55:04	2:17
2:18	1:24:19	1:29:35	1:34:52	1:40:08	1:45:24	1:50:40	1:55:56	2:18
2:19	1:24:48	1:30:06	1:35:24	1:40:42	1:46:00	1:51:18	1:56:36	2:19
2:20	1:25:26	1:30:47	1:36:07	1:41:28	1:46:48	1:52:08	1:57:29	2:20
2:21	1:26:05	1:31:28	1:36:50	1:42:13	1:47:36	1:52:59	1:58:22	2:21
2:22	1:26:43	1:32:08	1:37:34	1:42:59	1:48:24	1:53:49	1:59:14	2:22
2:23	1:27:22	1:32:49	1:38:17	1:43:44	1:49:12	1:54:40	2:00:07	2:23
2:24	1:28:00	1:33:30	1:39:00	1:44:30	1:50:00	1:55:30	2:01:00	2:24
2:25	1:28:29	1:34:06	1:39:32	1:45:04	1:50:36	1:56:08	2:01:40	2:25
2:26	1:29:07	1:34:41	1:40:16	1:45:50	1:51:24	1:56:58	2:02:32	2:26
2:27	1:29:46	1:35:22	1:40:59	1:46:35	1:52:12	1:57:49	2:03:25	2:27
2:28	1:30:24	1:36:03	1:41:42	1:47:21	1:53:00	1:58:39	2:04:18	2:28
2:29	1:31:02	1:36:44	1:42:25	1:48:07	1:53:48	1:59:29	2:05:11	2:29
2:30	1:31:41	1:37:25	1:43:08	1:48:52	1:54:36	2:00:20	2:06:04	2:30
2:35	1:34:43	1:40:38	1:46:34	1:52:29	1:58:24	2:04:19	2:10:14	2:35
2:40	1:37:46	1:43:52	1:49:59	1:56:05	2:02:12	2:08:19	2:14:25	2:40
2:45	1:40:48	1:47:06	1:53:24	1:59:42	2:06:00	2:12:18	2:18:36	2:45
2:50	1:43:50	1:50:20	1:56:49	2:03:19	2:09:48	2:16:17	2:22:47	2:50
2:55	1:46:53	1:53:34	2:00:14	2:06:55	2:13:36	2:20:17	2:26:58	2:55
3:00	1:49:55	1:56:47	2:03:40	2:10:32	2:17:24	2:24:16	2:31:08	3:00
3:15	1:59:02	2:06:29	2:13:55	2:21:22	2:28:48	2:36:14	2:43:41	3:15
3:30	2:08:19	2:16:20	2:24:22	2:32:23	2:40:24	2:48:25	2:56:26	3:30
3:45	2:17:26	2:26:02	2:34:37	2:43:13	2:51:48	3:00:23	3:08:59	3:45
4:00	2:26:34	2:35:43	2:44:53	2:54:02	3:03:12	3:12:22	3:21:31	4:00
4:15	2:35:41	2:45:25	2:55:08	3:04:52	3:14:36	3:24:20	3:34:04	4:15
4:30	2:44:48	2:55:06	3:05:24	3:15:42	3:26:00	3:36:18	3:44:24	4:30
4:45	2:54:05	3:05:58	3:15:50	3:26:43	3:37:36	3:48:29	3:59:22	4:45
5:00	3:03:12	3:14:39	3:26:06	3:37:33	3:49:00	4:00:27	4:11:54	5:00

*Times are rounded off to accommodate fractions of a second.

Mile	23	24	25	26	26.2		PACE
PACE							
2:04	1:48:47	1:53:31	1:58:15	2:02:59	2:03:56		2:04
2:05	1:49:42	1:54:29	1:59:15	2:04:12	2:04:58		2:05
2:06	1:50:38	1:55:26	2:00:15	2:05:06	2:06:00		2:06
2:07	1:51:32	1:56:23	2:01:14	2:06:05	2:07:00		2:07
2:08	1:52:27	1:57:21	2:02:14	2:07:06	2:08:00		2:08
2:09	1:53:10	1:58:05	2:03:00	2:07:55	2:08:55		2:09
2:10	1:54:05	1:59:02	2:04:00	2:08:57	2:09:57		2:10
2:11	1:55:00	2:00:00	2:05:00	2:10:00	2:11:00		2:11
2:12	1:55:52	2:00:54	2:05:56	2:11:02	2:12:00		2:12
2:13	1:56:48	2:01:50	2:06:55	2:12:00	2:13:00		2:13
2:14	1:57:32	2:02:38	2:07:45	2:12:52	2:13:53		2:14
2:15	1:58:27	2:03:36	2:08:45	2:13:54	2:14:56		2:15
2:16	1:59:22	2:04:34	2:09:45	2:14:56	2:15:59		2:16
2:17	2:00:17	2:05:31	2:10:43	2:15:57	2:17:00		2:17
2:18	2:01:13	2:06:28	2:11:42	2:16:55	2:18:00		2:18
2:19	2:01:54	2:07:12	2:12:30	2:17:48	2:18:58		2:19
2:20	2:02:49	2:08:10	2:13:30	2:18:50	2:19:55		2:20
2:21	2:03:44	2:09:07	2:14:30	2:19:53	2:20:57		2:21
2:22	2:04:40	2:10:05	2:15:30	2:20:55	2:22:00		2:22
2:23	2:05:35	2:11:02	2:16:30	2:21:58	2:23:00		2:23
2:24	2:06:30	2:12:00	2:17:30	2:23:00	2:24:00		2:24
2:25	2:07:11	2:12:43	2:18:15	2:23:47	2:24:53		2:25
2:26	2:08:07	2:13:41	2:19:15	2:24:49	2:25:56		2:26
2:27	2:09:02	2:14:38	2:20:15	2:25:52	2:26:59		2:27
2:28	2:09:57	2:15:36	2:21:15	2:26:54	2:28:00		2:28
2:29	2:10:52	2:16:34	2:22:15	2:27:56	2:29:00		2:29
2:30	2:11:46	2:17:28	2:23:12	2:28:55	2:30:00		2:30
2:35	2:16:10	2:22:05	2:28:00	2:33:55	2:35:00		2:35
2:40	2:20:32	2:26:38	2:32:42	2:38:48	2:40:00		2:40
2:45	2:24:54	2:31:12	2:37:30	2:43:48	2:45:00		2:45
2:50	2:29:16	2:35:46	2:42:15	2:48:44	2:50:00		2:50
2:55	2:33:38	2:40:19	2:47:00	2:53:41	2:55:00		2:55
3:00	2:38:06	2:44:53	2:51:45	2:58:37	3:00:00		3:00
3:15	2:51:07	2:58:34	3:06:00	3:13:26	3:15:00		3:15
3:30	3:04:28	3:12:29	3:20:30	3:28:31	3:30:00		3:30
3:45	3:17:34	3:26:10	3:34:45	3:43:20	3:45:00		3:45
4:00	3:30:41	3:39:50	3:49:00	3:58:10	4:00:00		4:00
4:15	3:43:47	3:53:31	4:03:15	4:12:59	4:15:00		4:15
4:30	3:56:54	4:07:12	4:17:30	4:27:48	4:30:00		4:30
4:45	4:10:14	4:21:07	4:32:00	4:42:53	4:45:00		4:45
5:00	4:23:21	4:47:48	4:46:15	4:57:42	5:00:00		5:00

*Times are rounded off to accommodate fractions of a second.

1997

JANUARY

S	M	T	W	T	F	S
			1	2	3	4
5	6	7	8	9	10	11
12	13	14	15	16	17	18
19	20	21	22	23	24	25
26	27	28	29	30	31	

FEBRUARY

S	M	T	W	T	F	S
						1
2	3	4	5	6	7	8
9	10	11	12	13	14	15
16	17	18	19	20	21	22
23	24	25	26	27	28	

MARCH

S	M	T	W	T	F	S
						1
2	3	4	5	6	7	8
9	10	11	12	13	14	15
16	17	18	19	20	21	22
23/30	24/31	25	26	27	28	29

APRIL

S	M	T	W	T	F	S
		1	2	3	4	5
6	7	8	9	10	11	12
13	14	15	16	17	18	19
20	21	22	23	24	25	26
27	28	29	30			

MAY

S	M	T	W	T	F	S
				1	2	3
4	5	6	7	8	9	10
11	12	13	14	15	16	17
18	19	20	21	22	23	24
25	26	27	28	29	30	31

JUNE

S	M	T	W	T	F	S
1	2	3	4	5	6	7
8	9	10	11	12	13	14
15	16	17	18	19	20	21
22	23	24	25	26	27	28
29	30					

JULY

S	M	T	W	T	F	S
		1	2	3	4	5
6	7	8	9	10	11	12
13	14	15	16	17	18	19
20	21	22	23	24	25	26
27	28	29	30	31		

AUGUST

S	M	T	W	T	F	S
					1	2
3	4	5	6	7	8	9
10	11	12	13	14	15	16
17	18	19	20	21	22	23
24/31	25	26	27	28	29	30

SEPTEMBER

S	M	T	W	T	F	S
	1	2	3	4	5	6
7	8	9	10	11	12	13
14	15	16	17	18	19	20
21	22	23	24	25	26	27
28	29	30				

OCTOBER

S	M	T	W	T	F	S
		1	2	3	4	
5	6	7	8	9	10	11
12	13	14	15	16	17	18
19	20	21	22	23	24	25
26	27	28	29	30	31	

NOVEMBER

S	M	T	W	T	F	S
						1
2	3	4	5	6	7	8
9	10	11	12	13	14	15
16	17	18	19	20	21	22
23/30	24	25	26	27	28	29

DECEMBER

S	M	T	W	T	F	S
	1	2	3	4	5	6
7	8	9	10	11	12	13
14	15	16	17	18	19	20
21	22	23	24	25	26	27
28	29	30	31